Flower Projects
for
All Occasions

Flower Projects

for

All Occasions

Joanna Sheen

PHOTOGRAPHY BY JACQUI HURST

CRESCENT BOOKS
NEW YORK • AVENEL

This 1995 edition published by Crescent Books,
distributed by Random House Value Publishing, Inc.
40 Engelhard Avenue, Avenel, New Jersey 07001

Random House
New York · Toronto · London · Sydney · Auckland

A CIP catalog record for this book is available from the Library of Congress.

By arrangement with Merehurst Limited, Ferry House
51–57 Lacy Road, Putney, London SW15 1PR

Text copyright © Joanna Sheen 1994
Photography & illustrations copyright © Merehurst Limited 1994

ISBN 0517 14014 4

Edited by **Heather Dewhurst**
Designed by **Lisa Tai**

Typeset by Servis Filmsetting Ltd, Manchester
Color separation by Global Color, Malaysia
Printed in Italy by Rotolito Lombarda

Contents

Introduction

Flowers have always been part of special occasions. Whether it is a wedding reception, a Christmas dinner, a birthday party, or a christening of a new baby, floral decorations add to the air of celebration. This book contains a wide range of inspirational flower projects to make, using fresh, dried, and pressed flowers, which are suitable for celebrations throughout the year.

The first chapter contains many ideas for weddings, with projects ranging from a lavish lily garland to a charming miniature bouquet.

The second chapter shows how to incorporate herbs into your arrangements for a more informal, country style, and includes baskets, wreaths, and even an unusual herbal horseshoe. Christmas is the subject of the third chapter, which contains plenty of creative ideas for decorating your home, tree, and even presents in a festive fashion. The final chapter contains ideas for floral gifts suitable for all occasions, from birthdays to Mother's Day.

I hope you are inspired by the ideas in this book and have fun arranging flowers for your own special occasions.

Chapter 1

Flowers for Celebrations

Flowers always play an important part in any celebration. Whether the occasion is a wedding or a birthday, some floral decorations will undoubtedly add to the success of the day.

If you are preparing flowers for a wedding, extra pairs of hands can often be a real help. It is a big undertaking to prepare wedding flowers, and the saying "Many hands make light work" can certainly be true. Plan your time like an army maneuver and all will go well – leave it until the last minute and everything may well go wrong! There are many occasions when you may want to have the expert help of a florist. But it is perfectly possible to do the flowers yourself if you have the time and the inclination. These projects should help you decide what you would like to make and show you how to create your decorations with the minimum of trouble.

Special occasions can be great fun and very hard work – but as much enjoyment can be derived from the preparations as from the actual day!

Country flower basket

This delightful arrangement is ideal for an informal party or buffet. It brings the garden indoors and creates the effect of abundance. You can change the fruit or the color of the flowers for different effects.

Country flower basket

An informal display of daisies, fruit, and vegetables, this arrangement is fairly simple and yet rather different. The vegetables and fruit cannot be re-used, since they have been wired, but they make a pleasant change from the more typical basket containing only flowers and foliage. You will need two bunches of white daisy spray, approximately 20 fresh string beans, about 1½ pound (750 g) Brussels sprouts, 1 pound (500 g) kale, and 6 to 8 green apples – although other alternatives could be substituted.

INGREDIENTS

4 terracotta or plastic flowerpots, 4 inches (10cm) in diameter

3 pieces of green floral foam

Flowers, fruit, and vegetables, see above

Plastic wrap

A shallow basket, 18 inches (45cm) long

Medium-gauge florist's wires

Small, pointed wooden sticks

ॐ

1 Fill the flowerpots with pre-soaked floral foam. Arrange the daisies in the pots to resemble growing plants. Make sure the foam is wet, but not so wet that the pots drip. Line the basket with plastic wrap.

2 *Place the rest of the wet foam in the basket. Arrange the stems of kale in the foam as you would foliage. Place the pots of daisies in the arrangement. If they keep falling, insert a stub wire through the pots and into the foam in the basket to secure them.*

3 *Wire the Brussels sprouts by pushing the wire halfway through and then twisting the "legs" of the wire together; bunch two or three together. Make small bundles of string beans, and push the sticks into the base of the apples. Add groups of Brussels sprouts, beans, and apples in each side of the arrangement.*

13

Pew end

This decoration can be hung vertically or horizontally, or simply laid on a table. It has so many more uses besides the pew end it was originally designed to be! Because the ingredients are all either dried or preserved, the arrangement will last for ages.

$\mathscr{P}$ew end

Using a piece of hardboard as a base is inexpensive and gives the arrangement many differing uses. Fit the hardboard with a D ring picture hook to hang it vertically or 2 D rings with wire between to hang horizontally. If you intend to place the arrangement on a table, obviously no fixings should be added, in case they scratch the table. You will need a small bunch of preserved foliage such as oak and copper beech leaves, a bunch of orange carthamus, 3 large red hydrangea heads, 6 bell cups, a selection of artificial fruit and berries, some hazelnuts, dried red chilies, and a bunch of red roses.

INGREDIENTS

Flowers, fruit, and foliage, see above

Piece of hardboard, approximately 18 × 6 inches (45 × 15 cm)

Glue gun and glue

D rings as required

ð

1 Cut small sprays of the preserved foliage, and arrange them alternately around the edge of the hardboard, so that you have a complete border of leaves around the hardboard and a bare center. Glue the foliage in place.

2 *Glue individual carthamus heads between the leaves toward the edge of the arrangement. Add the hydrangea heads, broken down if necessary, and the bell cups, arranged so that they zigzag down the center of the display. Fill the bell cups with hazelnuts, gluing them in individually.*

3 *Attach the bunches of berries and artificial fruits between the other ingredients, then add the chilies either singly or in small groups, depending on their size. Finally, add the red roses in clumps of three or five. Once the glue has dried, fit the pew end with D rings, as required.*

Welcome wreath

This ring of flowers would look stunning as a welcoming arrangement for a summer party, barbecue, or autumnal gathering. You will need a bunch of pale pink dried peonies (I have used "Sarah Bernhardt" peonies), a bunch of 20 pink roses (these are called "Souvenir"), a small bunch of pink baby's breath, a few ears of wheat, and some preserved oak leaves.

INGREDIENTS

Glue gun and glue

Flowers and foliage

Wreath base, 10–12 inches (25–30cm) in diameter

3½ yards (3m) ribbon, 2 inches (5cm) wide

Fine-gauge floral wire

2¼ yards (2m) chiffon ribbon, 1½ inches (4cm) wide

Scissors

❧

1 Glue the leaves around the wreath. Add some ears of wheat. Using the wider ribbon, make a generous bow by wiring across a figure eight (see diagram on page 131), and leave long tails on the bow. Attach this to the ring with wire, and then make a smaller bow with the chiffon ribbon; attach that on top of the plain ribbon.

2 Glue on the peonies, having removed all but 1 inch (2·5 cm) of their stems. Finally remove all the leaves from the roses, and cut the stems down to about 2–3 inches (5–8cm). Then glue the roses into the arrangement, making sure to place them evenly around the ring.

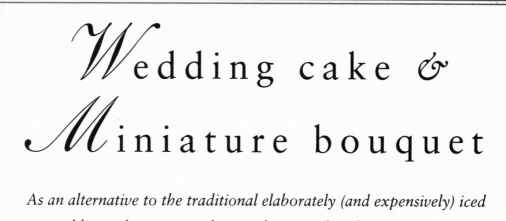

Wedding cake & Miniature bouquet

As an alternative to the traditional elaborately (and expensively) iced wedding cake, try your favorite homemade cake, spectacularly bedecked with fresh flowers. The nosegay adds a special touch to a place setting or gift.

Wedding cake

There are very few who could undertake to ice a wedding cake in the approved professional manner, whereas decorating with flowers, although it involves a little patience and planning, should be beyond the skills of no one. The flowers can obviously be varied according to your color scheme, but make sure to include something frothy like baby's breath, as it lightens the design beautifully. Here I used a bunch of cream lilies, a bunch of peach roses, a little foliage, some baby's breath, and a bunch of cream Singapore orchids.

INGREDIENTS

Wedding cake – in this case a 10-inch (25cm) base with a 7-inch (18cm) top tier

Flowers and foliage, see above

Fine-gauge floral wire

Green floral tape

10 inches (25cm) cream ribbon

1 Make sure the cake boards are quite a bit bigger than the cakes, to allow room for the flowers. A plain base with a minimal amount of decoration will suffice, but you can have more if you prefer. Before you start decorating the cake, put the pillars in position and mark the place, so that you can reassemble the cake accurately if necessary. Make small flower bunches with either a lily or a rose in each, together with a few other ingredients. Wire them together, then cover the wire and stems with green floral tape. Each bunch should be no more than 3–4 inches (8–10cm) long.

2 *Once you have made up some bunches, try arranging them against the lower tier of the cake. They should all be roughly the same size, or it becomes difficult to achieve the right effect. Lay one bunch over another, making sure that the wired ends are well covered by another flower. Place a spray at each end of the side of the cake, and work toward the middle to camouflage the stems.*

3 *Make a larger bunch of flowers for the top of the cake, cover the stems with cream ribbon, and tie it in a pretty bow. Now assemble the cake in its final position and place the flowers on the cake. If necessary, you can cover one or two problem areas with individual flowers rather than entire bunches.*

*M*iniature bouquet

This nosegay is quick and easy to make and would be a wonderful alternative to the more usual table decorations. The silver doily can be bought from good stationery stores; alternatively you could spray a paper doily with silver or gold paint and use that. You will need 5 flowers from a bunch of spray carnations, a small amount of baby's breath, 7 ivy leaves and 7 small cones such as alder or larch.

INGREDIENTS

Flowers and foliage, see above

Fine-gauge floral wire

A silver doily or sprayed doily

Ribbons, optional

Glue gun and glue

Green floral tape (optional)

1 *Place a carnation in the center and make a bunch with baby's breath and the other carnations. Wrap this firmly with wire, leaving a piece about 10 inches (25cm) long for finishing the* bouquet. *It is important to use long-lasting flowers as they must look fresh throughout the celebration. Carnations are a good choice, for they do not wilt too quickly.*

2 *Place the ivy leaves around the edge of the bouquet, and wrap the wire firmly around them. Other individual leaves could be substituted if ivy is not available. The bouquet could be left as it is and the ivy leaves used as the frill if you prefer.*

3 *Push the stems through the doily, and tie some ribbons around it if you wish. Using a hot glue gun, glue the small cones in place among the flowers. I think it looks pretty to leave the stems as they are; however, if you prefer, you could wrap them with green floral tape.*

Rose & lily
centerpiece

This small, cheerful arrangement would be ideal for the center of a buffet table in a large function room. The terracotta base is fairly inexpensive and can be found at garden centers, while the flowers can be chosen from those available in the garden at the time.

Rose & lily centerpiece

This table decoration could be altered to suit any color scheme, depending upon your choice for the occasion. The base is the saucer that is usually provided with a flowerpot. In this case it was bought separately for a very reasonable amount. The floral foam should be well soaked so that the arrangement lasts as long as possible. Make sure the foliage has been cut from the garden the night before and soaked in a bucket overnight. You will need some greenery from the garden, a bunch of cream lilies, and a bunch of peach roses.

INGREDIENTS

A block of green floral foam

Terracotta plant pot saucer, 5 inches (13cm) in diameter

Green floral tape (optional)

Flowers and foliage, see above

Scissors

1 Having soaked the foam well, cut it to fit tightly into the saucer. If you wish to secure it further you can use green floral tape around the foam and under the saucer.

Insert some pieces of greenery into the foam to cover it well; a mixture of different varieties of foliage looks quite charming.

2 Cut down the bunch of lilies, making several small sprays; the more open lilies can be used individually. Place them around the arrangement, putting the tighter buds toward the edge of the display and the more open flowers slightly farther in toward the center.

3 Finally, add the peach roses to the arrangement. If you make sure that they have had a long drink before you use them, the centerpiece should last very well indeed. If you wanted to make a less expensive centerpiece, you could substitute peachy/bronze chrysanthemums or peach spray carnations for the roses.

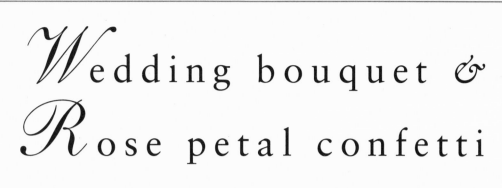

Wedding bouquet & Rose petal confetti

A complicated wedding bouquet is definitely a job for a trained florist, but this tied bunch is simple to make and gives the bride a beautiful armful of flowers to carry. Homemade confetti is far prettier than the colored paper variety and very easy to make.

Wedding bouquet

This beautiful bouquet is fairly simple to make, and provided you have practiced a few times before the day with some less expensive flowers or flowers from the garden, you should be able to master this project. It is important to use pretty ribbons; however, if the budget does not stretch to satin or wired ribbons, choose the most neutral color, such as cream or white, so that the ribbon is not too obvious. An inexpensive paper ribbon would be fine. For the bouquet you will need 10 stems of cream lilies, some foliage such as pussy willow and phormium leaves, and some baby's breath.

INGREDIENTS

Flowers and foliage, see above

Fine-gauge floral wire

3½ yards (3m) ribbon, 3 inches (8cm) wide

3½ yards (3m) ribbon, 2 inches (5cm) wide

3½ yards (3m) ribbon, 1 inch (2.5cm) wide

ε૪

1 Make sure all the flowers and foliage have been well conditioned before you use them. Place some long pieces of pussy willow in a fan shape. Add in some more foliage and a big piece of baby's breath. Wire this together firmly to make a base for your bouquet.

2 *Continue by adding stems of lilies into your bunch, wiring every few stems as you go. Keep the fan shape of the bunch, and make sure the lilies are well distributed. Bring some of the flower* heads well down the length of the bouquet. Check the bouquet from all angles; make sure you have used a reasonable amount of baby's breath as this lightens the bouquet. Add more greenery *as you wish. Once you are satisfied with your bunch, wrap a piece of wire firmly around the bunch a few times to secure it.*

3 *Take the widest ribbon and tie it around the bouquet to make a pretty bow with trailing ends. Then repeat with the medium width of ribbon, taking the ends across the wide bow and tying. This will give you a double bow. Then finish the bouquet with the narrowest ribbon, again tying the ends across the other two bows to give an even more splendid effect.*

$\mathcal{R}$ose petal confetti

Dried rose petals have a fairly long life if you keep them warm and in the dark, so you could start planning and making your confetti several months before the wedding. Either garden roses or commercial roses can be used. Red roses keep their color far better than any other rose, but other varieties will all add to the blend of colors in the confetti. Make sure that you store them in a damp-proof box in a warm atmosphere.

INGREDIENTS

Bunches of roses

Airtight container

Rose essential oil (optional)

1 Hang the bunches of roses in a warm, dry place. Make sure each bunch is secured with a rubber band and not string, for the stems will shrink during the drying period. Alternatively, you can dry the rose petals individually by placing them on a cake rack in a warm room. It is best not to collect old rose petals that have fallen to the ground, or you may find that most of them turn brown when they are dry, as they may be too old.

2 Once the bunch of roses seems completely dry, remove all the petals from the roses and store them in an airtight container. You may choose to keep the different colors separate or to mix them from the beginning. You will need the petals from quite a large number of roses to be able to shower a bride in a small cascade of confetti.

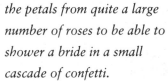

3 Once the petals are in the container, keep them well sealed and warm. As an extra touch, you could add a drop or two of rose essential oil to intensify the scent, but do not add too much or it will become overpowering. The dried petals should keep for several months.

Circlet of flowers

Although a reasonable amount of wiring skill is needed for this project, with time and practice this can be achieved. It is important to use simple, robust flowers and to handle the flowers as gently, but firmly as possible.

Circlet of flowers

It takes a little extra practice and skill to make this wired headdress, but if you experiment with some garden flowers first, you may well find it easier than you imagined. Try to handle the flowers gently, or they will become bruised and the edges will turn brown. Any foliage is suitable, but ivy is particularly good, as it lasts fairly well out of water and makes a pretty dark foil for the roses. Measure the circumference of the child's head with a piece of narrow ribbon or string and bend the wires to that exact size. You will need a bunch of pink roses, ivy, and some baby's breath. I have used preserved baby's breath which has been tinted pink to complement the roses – it is also much tougher than fresh baby's breath.

INGREDIENTS

4 × heavy-gauge floral wires, 12 inches (30cm) long

Green floral tape

Flowers and foliage, see above

Fine-gauge floral wire

3½ yards (3m) ribbon

❧

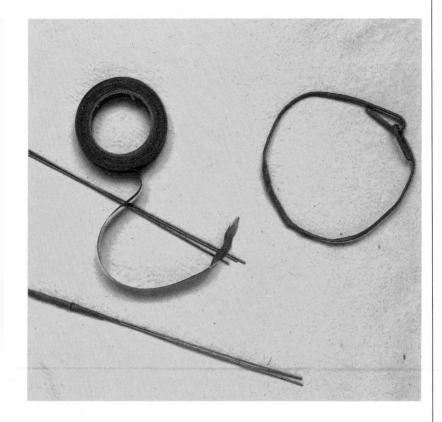

1 *Having carefully measured the circumference of the child's head, use two wires together to lay out the required length. Overlap the two or three lengths of wire you may require, and allow 1 inch (2.5cm) or so more for the hooks at each end. Wrap the wires tightly in green floral tape. Make a loop at each end of the wires, and interlock them as you gently bend them around into a circle.*

2 *Make small bunches of your chosen ingredients, including a piece of foliage, a rose and some baby's breath, and wire them at the base. Then attach the bunches to the wire ring, using either wire or the green floral tape.*

3 *Place some bunches on each side of the wire and some on top. Continue around the ring until it is completely covered. Tie the ribbon around the sparsest point of* the headdress. Knot it firmly and tie a bow with long streamers – this will be the back of the headdress. One or two colors of ribbon can be used, depending on the color scheme of the dress. The finished headdress can either be balanced on the head or held with barrettes.

Lily garland

A garland is a time-consuming project to make, but the finished effect is lovely and can be used in many different ways. A doorway can be decorated with the garland above it or a gateway can have a garland twisted through it. This fresh garland could be hung outside or indoors – it would make a wonderful decoration for a fireplace or sideboard for a summer celebration. You will need (depending upon the finished length you require) 10 stems of pink lilies, a bunch of white daisy spray, a bunch of pink daisy spray, and plenty of foliage.

INGREDIENTS

2¼ yards (2m) cord or twisted paper ribbon

Fine-gauge floral wire

Flowers and foliage, see above

A reel of green floral tape

Ribbons if desired, 1 yard (1m) per bow

❧

1 Make a loop to hang the garland at each end of the cord or paper ribbon, and wire it firmly. Make small sprays of the various ingredients. Wire each spray at the base. Then, using green floral tape, attach them to the cord or ribbon, starting at each end. Keep the bunches well spaced so that the garland does not become over-full.

2 When you reach the middle, overlap the stems as completely as possible, and then cover any gaps by adding individual flowers. Wire a large bow to the center of the garland if desired. Ribbons can also be added in a similar fashion at each end if you wish.

Presentation bouquet

Flowers are always a lovely way of saying thank you to someone. This little bouquet is simple to make, yet with its frill of handmade paper it is delightfully different.

$\mathcal{P}$resentation bouquet

This bouquet could be made as a hostess gift or as a thank-you for someone who has helped or spoken at a public occasion. The frill around the bouquet and the bow are both constructed from Japanese tissue paper. If you cannot obtain this paper, use ordinary tissue or handmade paper in a thin tissue version. Any of these makes a refreshing change from the more formal effect of cellophane. You will need a bunch of pink spray carnations and a bunch of pink alstroemeria. For the foliage I used telima leaves, picked in their fall coloring, but you could substitute any other large individual leaves to go among the flowers.

INGREDIENTS

Flowers and foliage, see above

Fine-gauge floral wires

Scissors

A sheet of Japanese tissue paper

Pin or glue

❧

1 Make a small bunch with an open carnation in the center, surrounded by alstroemeria and more carnations. Bind the stems with the wires, keeping the binding to a minimum and in one position only. Make sure that the flowers have been in water for at least a few hours, preferably overnight, before using them.

2 Add more flowers and the telima leaves to the bouquet. There is no need to bind each ingredient in individually; simply wrap the wire around the stems once you have added three or four pieces. For a neater effect, keep the wire binding in the same position rather than traveling up and down the stems.

3 Cut a 3-inch (8cm) wide strip from the longest edge of the paper to act as the ribbon. Cut a large square from the remaining paper, and fold it in half and then in quarters to make a triangle. Snip a small triangle from the end to make a hole. Slide the flowers through this hole, and fix the paper around them with a couple of twists of wire. Tie the "ribbon" into a bow, and fix it to the bouquet with a large pin or some glue.

Long table decoration

For most celebrations the top table is usually a long, rectangular shape, which lends itself well to a trailing arrangement in the center or front. If the table is very large, two similar arrangements strategically placed would look excellent.

Long table decoration

The shape of this arrangement is ideal for a rectangular or oval table or, alternatively, for a sideboard or cabinet. It is important never to leave the room with the candles alight, for the foliage could easily catch fire and spoil your celebrations. You will need a bunch of 9 small red gerbera, a few stems of golden rod, assorted greenery, and about a dozen pieces of fruit, such as apples and passion fruit. If possible, use some herbal foliage, as this will add a subtle aroma.

INGREDIENTS

A block of green floral foam

A dinner plate

Floral tape

Medium–heavy gauge florist's wires

Sticky tape

3 candles

Flowers and foliage, see above

Small, pointed wooden sticks

A selection of fruit

❧

1 Place the soaked foam on the plate and fix it firmly to the plate with floral tape. Take 9 pieces of wire, about 3–4 inches (8–10cm) long, and bend them into the shape of hairpins. Tape three of these hairpins around each candle to act as supports, and push them into the foam. Cover the foam with the pieces of assorted greenery.

2 *Insert the gerbera and small pieces of golden rod on all sides of the arrangement, making sure that the base of the candles and all the foam are well covered.*

3 *Push a wooden stick into each piece of fruit that you wish to use, and add the fruit to the arrangement, making sure that it is firmly fixed in place. The fruit will deteriorate fairly rapidly, because it has been damaged, but it should last well through a festive weekend or few days.*

Arranging flowers for special occasions

Organization and forward planning are the keys to a successful celebration. This applies to the flowers as much as to any other aspect of the occasion. Order the flowers you think you will need from a local florist well before the occasion; if you are making a garland or a bouquet for the first time, do a trial run to see how long it will take. It is all too easy to underestimate the time that floral arrangements can take – twenty minutes before you need them will not do!

Good-quality fresh flowers are the key to longer-lasting arrangements. As a general rule, flowers should be cut across the stalk diagonally and immersed in deep water overnight before being used in an arrangement. This will give them a good drink, and help them last longer. If your arrangements allow, re-cut the stems and change the water regularly. If the arrangement is in wet foam, keep the water level topped up so that the foam does not dry out.

Using dried flowers for your decorations would remove any wilting or drooping problems, but they do not always fit into the overall scheme of decorations. Silk flowers are another, albeit expensive, alternative that might solve some problems.

BOUQUETS & HEADDRESSES

If you decide to try making your own or a friend's bridal bouquet or headdress, try to choose flowers that will last fairly well out of water. There are many varieties, especially some garden flowers, that would last barely long enough to make it to the reception. Some varieties, however, will last far better than others when kept without water – for example, carnations, lilies, roses, gypsophila (baby's breath), and most varieties of foliage.

Try to handle the flowers as little as possible, and keep them cool and damp until required. Even the best-quality, freshest bloom will tire and bruise with heavy handling. Wiring should be kept to a minimum. If you fancy a very elaborate design that needs a great deal of wiring I suggest that you get a professional florist to do the job for you, so that you can be sure your flowers will look perfect for the important day.

FLOWERS FOR ROOMS AND HALLS

If you are arranging flowers in a church or hotel, or anyone's property (even your own!), try to work cleanly and tidily. A couple of large plastic garbage bags are very handy, and an old sheet to stand and work on is also an excellent way to prevent any damage to carpets and lessen the time spent in clearing up. Lay the sheet out in the area where you wish to work, and keep all your flowers and tools on that sheet. When you have finished, place any large pieces of refuse, such as stems and large leaves, in the plastic bags, and carefully bundle up the sheet and carry it outside. Small stems and petals can then simply be tipped straight onto a compost heap or into a garbage can.

If you are planning to arrange wedding flowers in a church or hotel, make sure to ask for permission before starting your arrangements – some churches have very definite ideas about their floral

decorations, and a hotel may have certain guide-lines concerning the size or placing of flower arrangements on the premises.

Good-quality flowers and assorted ribbons and wires are the basic ingredients of most arrangements.

MEMENTOS OF THE OCCASION

There are several ways that you could make your occasion even more memorable with flowers. One idea is to make a simple nosegay for each of the ladies to take home – these take very little time to prepare. Alternatively, you could make small table gifts by filling sachets with dried lavender or pot-pourri and then tying the neck of the sachet with some ribbon and a couple of flowers.

You could also dry some of the flowers after-ward to preserve those special memories. Roses are very easy to dry and are often included in special-occasion arrangements. Choose some blooms that are not too open or bruised, and

group them in bunches of six or seven with a rubber band. Hang the bunches in a warm, dark spot, where they will dry within a week or two, depending on the heat in the room, and will be ready to use. You could then make a lovely dried-flower arrangement to keep as a lasting memento of the day.

I hope you enjoy arranging flowers for your special celebration. I have had tremendous fun both as an over-enthusiastic amateur and as a pro-fessional in decorating for dances, weddings, and parties. It gives you a marvelous sense of achieve-ment when you see how pretty the flowers look on the day.

CHAPTER 2

Herbs & Flowers

Herbs have played an important part in the everyday life of mankind for centuries – they can decorate, heal, soothe, and enhance the flavor of food, which makes them one of the most valuable groups of plants that you could grow in your garden. If you are short of garden space, you can purchase many herbs fresh or still growing in pots from supermarkets and delicatessens.

The beautiful soft grays and blues associated with many herbs make them a joy to look at in the garden and a useful palette of colors to mix with other flowers and plants in decorations and arrangements. Herbs should never be considered too humble to play a part in celebrations and special occasions. The magic power of herbs has given them a position of respect throughout history, and they were always part of important occasions. Whether you use herbs in a small way, such as including some rosemary in a bridal bouquet, or give them a larger role, such as decorating tables in mixed herb arrangements, herbs always look attractive.

Basket of herbs

This rustic gardening basket of herbs and daisies will last well, as the flowers are in plenty of water and the herbs in pots. It would make a lovely display for a kitchen window or table, and the herbs can be used for cooking when needed.

$\mathcal{B}$asket of herbs

This is a very informal basket arrangement which would look charming on a kitchen table and can come in very handy when you need a sprig of basil or parsley. Herbs do not stay fresh in an arrangement for long, so this is the perfect answer – potted herbs together with flowers in separate containers of water. For this arrangement you will need a selection of abundant potted herbs – I have used 4 pots of basil, 3 pots of parsley, 2 pots of purple sage, and some small white daisies.

INGREDIENTS

Herbs and flowers, see above

A gardening basket, approximately 14 inches (35cm) long

2 jam jars

Cut-flower food (optional)

❧

1 Make sure the pots of basil have been well watered, then position them in the basket.

Never use weak or spindly specimens, as they will spoil the overall effect.

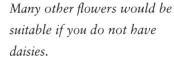

2 Fill the jam jars with water and, if you wish, some cut-flower food. Place some sprays of small white daisies in the jars at varying heights. Add the daisies to the basket.

Many other flowers would be suitable if you do not have daisies.

3 Position the pots of parsley and sage to fill the basket. Try to choose herbs that contrast in color as well as in leaf shape and texture, to achieve the best combination.

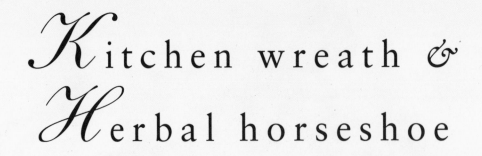

Kitchen wreath & Herbal horseshoe

This wreath is perfect for the kitchen with its amusing addition of wine corks and pots of beans. The horseshoe would make an unusual good luck token for a bride – it's fairly heavy but it looks lovely!

$\mathscr{K}$itchen wreath

With kitchen space often at a premium, this herbal decoration is ideal for hanging on the wall or a cabinet door, where it won't take up any counter space. The bay leaves can be used fresh and allowed to dry in position, or used once they have dried out. You will also need some wheat, box leaves, marjoram, sage, and a large hydrangea head. Finally, you will need to drink a few bottles of wine to collect the corks necessary for the decoration, but that may not be too great a hardship!

INGREDIENTS

Herbs and flowers, see above

Glue gun and glue

A wreath base, 8 inches (20cm) in diameter

6 miniature flowerpots

Kidney beans, mung beans, and navy beans

❧

1 *Glue the bay leaves either individually or in sprays onto the wreath base, making a curve that covers about two-thirds of the ring. Cut the* ears of wheat so that their stems are very short, and place a small group on each side of the wreath on the bay leaves. Glue in place.

2 *Place the corks in the middle of the decorated curve, gluing them on individually. Add some sprays of box on either side of the corks. Then add some small sprays of dried gray sage and bunches of marjoram, leaving some gaps for the terracotta flowerpots to fill.*

3 *Once you feel the wreath is full enough, add the little flowerpots, three on each side of the corks. Glue the dried beans into the pots. If you have not got these particular pulses, you could use lentils, pasta, other varieties of dried herbs, or small pieces of dried fruit.*

Herbal horseshoe

A horseshoe is meant to bring good luck and makes a lovely wedding gift or good luck token. This horseshoe is one from a local horse, but if you have trouble finding real horseshoes try asking a riding stable and they may be able to help you. The shoe will need cleaning before you use it – plenty of sandpaper and elbow grease to remove any rust, and metal cleaner to bring out the shine. Then give the horseshoe a coat of varnish to prevent any further rusting. For the decoration you will need bay leaves, some sprays of boxwood leaves, and 7 or 8 small pink roses.

INGREDIENTS

Raffia

Horseshoe

Glue gun and glue

Flowers and foliage, see above

Cinnamon sticks

Fine-gauge floral wires

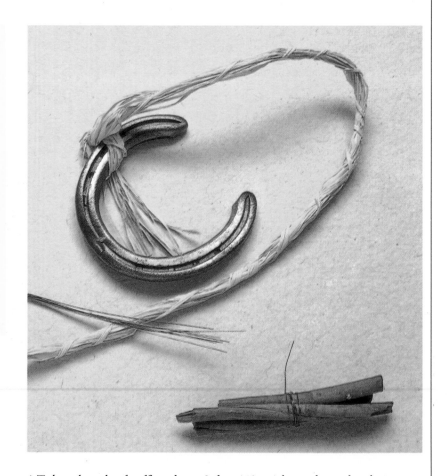

1 Take a length of raffia, about 2 feet (60cm) long, from the skein, and twist it until it resembles a thick cord. If it is a little unmanageable, twist a separate strand of raffia around it to hold it together. Knot the raffia around both ends of the horseshoe, and glue it at the back to ensure that it stays in place. Glue a small raffia bow to the center of the twisted raffia strand for added decoration.

2 *Glue some sprays of bay to each side of the center of the shoe, and add some small sprays of boxwood. Other green herbs or foliage could be used if you cannot find either of these varieties. Make a small bundle of cinnamon sticks by wrapping wire around them.*

3 *Wrap raffia around the cinnamon bundle to conceal the wire, and glue it to the center of the horseshoe. Finally glue the roses to each side of the cinnamon.*

Teacup of herbs

This lovely arrangement of fresh herbs and pansies can be made in a very short time, perhaps using ingredients from your garden. The finished project is charming and would delight anyone as a gift or as a decoration for a summer tea table. You will need a selection of herbs, such as rosemary, rue (Jackman's Blue), gray sage, and some small violas or a selection of pansies.

INGREDIENTS

Scissors

Green floral foam

A cup and saucer

Flowers and herbs, see above

Fine-gauge floral wire (optional)

Narrow purple ribbon, approximately 12 inches (30cm) long

෨

1 Cut the foam so that it is fractionally larger than the diameter of the cup, and press it in firmly. Soak the foam with water. Insert a selection of herbs into the foam all around the cup, making sure to cover the foam completely.

2 Carefully add the violas to the arrangement. Their stalks are very soft, so they tend to break easily; if you find it impossible to push the stalks into the foam, gently wrap some fine floral wire around the stems to strengthen them. To complete the display, make a tiny bunch of the herbs and flowers used in the teacup, and tie it with the purple ribbon. This nosegay could then be laid on a matching saucer.

Topiary trees & Herbs in terracotta

These herbal topiary trees would make a lovely decoration for any room. The fresh herbs in terracotta are brightened by the addition of chili peppers and kumquats.

Topiary trees

These tiny topiary trees are really gorgeous and will make a very attractive centerpiece or windowsill decoration. Although they look impressive, they are relatively easy to make. Most herbs can be used but avoid the softer herbs, such as basil, which might not last so well. To make a topiary tree, you will need a large bunch of thyme and a cinnamon stick for each tree, plus the herb of your choice. Here I used curry plant foliage for the medium-sized tree and golden sage for the largest tree.

INGREDIENTS

A small terracotta container

2 pieces of green floral foam

Cinnamon stick, approximately 6 inches (15cm) long

Knife

Herb of your choice

Ribbon or small flowers for decoration (optional)

1 If there is a hole in the container, drop in a piece of cardboard to cover it. Fill the container with foam and soak well. Push the cinnamon stick into the foam and place the second piece of foam on top. Cut the corners off this piece to produce a rounded shape.

2 Cover the base with a selection of greenery or the single herb used for the ball of the tree. Place pieces of herb at each side and at the top of the foam ball to produce the outer points of your circular shape.

3 Fill in the rest of the ball with small pieces of thyme, placed either singly or in small groups. Keep turning *the tree as you are filling in the gaps so that the overall shape is as round as possible. Once the tree is complete,* *you could add more decoration, such as a ribbon or small flowerheads.*

Herbs in terracotta

Herbs make a delightful subject for an informal kitchen arrangement. Here herbs and some vegetables and fruit have been combined for an unusual combination. Any other small vegetables could be substituted. The foliage and herbs can come from your garden or from a selection at the supermarket and florist's. You will need 7 or 8 pieces of bay, 7 large ivy leaves, and a bunch of rue (such as Jackman's Blue).

INGREDIENTS

Terracotta pot

Piece of green floral foam

Small bundle of medium–heavy gauge florist's wires

1 small cauliflower or broccoli

10 or more asparagus tips

7 kumquats

❧

1 Fill the terracotta pot with foam and soak well. Add the bay sprigs around the pot so that they almost cover the foam. Other medium-leaved greenery such as scented geranium leaves, could be used instead.

2 Add the ivy leaves to the pot. If they have strong stems, you can place them straight into the foam; if the stems are too flexible to do this, strengthen them with some wire wrapped around the stem. The foam should be completely covered by now.

3 Add the rue throughout the arrangement. Then wire the pieces of cauliflower by pushing a wire halfway through the stalk and twisting the two ends together to make a wire stem. Wire the asparagus and kumquats in the same way. Place these ingredients in the arrangement to complete the design.

Bath sachets & Potpourri

Bath sachets filled with herbs from the garden will give you a soothing, relaxing bath. The herbal potpourri is also made with garden produce and is much prettier than commercial varieties.

$\mathcal{B}$ath sachets

Using bath sachets is a lovely old-fashioned way of scenting your bath water, and makes a lovely change from bright pink bubble bath! You can use any number of herbal mixtures inside the bag – lavender is always successful, as is fresh or dried rosemary. Dried roses or rosebuds are also a useful standby. If you want to strengthen the scent and the relaxing effect of the herbal bath, add a few drops of the matching essential oil to the water.

INGREDIENTS

Scissors

Unbleached muslin

Herbs of your choice

Small rubber bands

Ribbon or cord

1 Cut some squares of muslin – about 9 inches (23cm) wide seems to be a workable size. If the pieces are cut any smaller, *you will not be able to fit the herbs inside. As an alternative to unbleached muslin, you could use lawn or batiste.*

2 *Lay a few sprigs of your chosen herbs in the center of the square of fabric, gather up the sides and secure with a rubber band. It is just as easy to make several bags at a time, and they can sit in a basket or bowl by the bathtub until they are needed.*

3 *Cut some long pieces of ribbon and tie them around each rubber band, adding a small bow if desired. The ends of the ribbon can then be tied around the faucets so that the bag dangles in the water. When the faucets are turned on to fill the tub, the stream of water will pass through the sachet and perfume your bath.*

$\mathscr{P}$otpourri

Making your own potpourri is always fun, and herbs make very good potpourri components. You can dry the herbs by placing them on a paper towel and cooking them in the microwave on medium to full power for 2 minutes. Any herbal foliage can be used as the leaf base of this mixture; the dominant scent will be provided by the essential oil(s) used. Here I used one cup of each of the following: rue leaves; angelica leaves; lemon balm; dark pink, scented rose petals; mixed pieces of spice – cloves, cinnamon, and nutmeg; and lavender flowers. In addition you need ½ ounce (15g) orrisroot, 1 tsp any herbal essential oil or perfume oil (I used a mixture of marjoram and lavender), and a few small sprays of lavender to decorate.

INGREDIENTS

Potpourri ingredients, see above

Bowl

Metal spoon

Large plastic bag

Rubber band

Container for potpourri

Shells

Glue

❧

1 *Dry all the necessary ingredients and mix together in a bowl with the orrisroot and oil. Stir well, using a metal spoon (a wooden spoon would absorb the oil).*

2 Tip the mixture into a large plastic bag and secure the top with a rubber band. Shake well and leave for a week or so to mature. The scents will blend together and smell far better if you are patient!

3 While the potpourri is maturing, decorate a plain container in which you can display your potpourri. Choose a container with a smooth surface (old Camembert cheese boxes work well), and glue on shells in a random design to cover it completely. Alternatively, you could decorate the box with spices or dried seed pods.

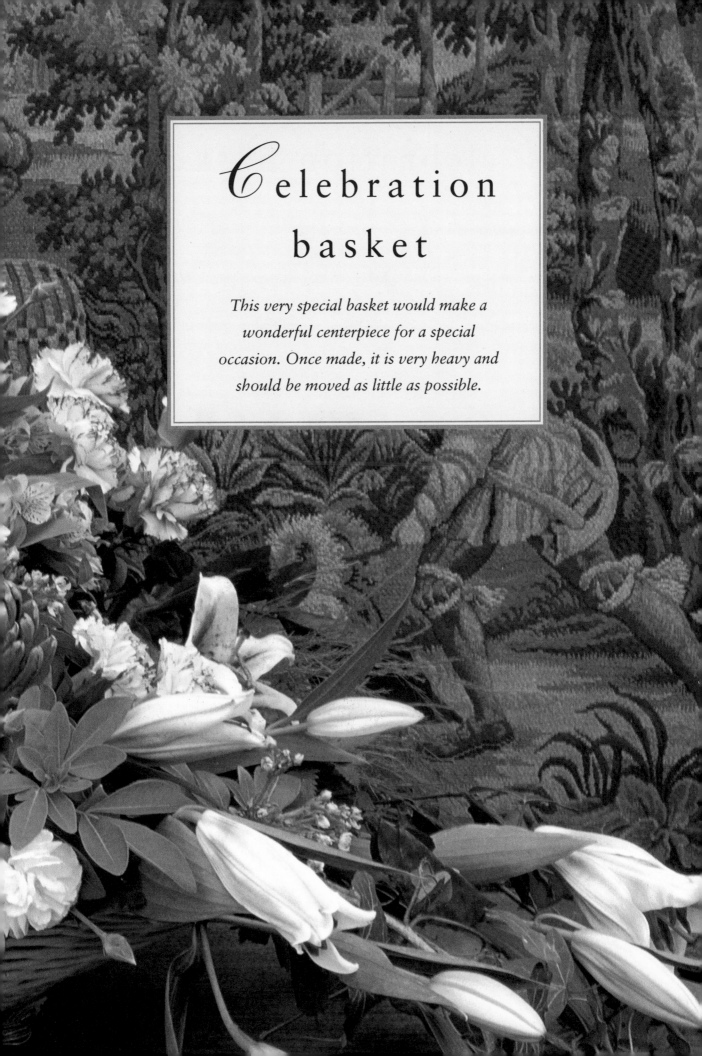

Celebration basket

This very special basket would make a wonderful centerpiece for a special occasion. Once made, it is very heavy and should be moved as little as possible.

Celebration basket

This magnificent arrangement is for a very special occasion and could be placed on the floor, on a side table, or on the edge of a platform. Although this is a very large arrangement, such items as bunches of grapes and artichokes can take up large amounts of the space and therefore save money on the flower content of the basket. To make this celebration basket you will need 2 bunches (10 stems) of stargazer lilies, a bunch of white spray carnations, 2 bunches of striped carnations, a bunch of white alstroemeria, and 30 assorted stems of herbal and other greenery, including trails of ivy.

INGREDIENTS

Shallow basket, about 18 inches (45cm) long

Plastic sheeting to fit basket

4 blocks of green floral foam

Floral tape

Foliage and flowers, see above

1 large bunch of purple grapes, 3 limes, 3 plums, 3 green apples, 3 globe artichoke heads, 3 purple and green kohlrabi or small purple-tinged turnips

Pointed wooden sticks, approximately 12 inches (30cm) long

❧

1 Line the basket carefully with the plastic, and insert four well-soaked blocks of foam. Tape the blocks firmly to the plastic so that they do not move about. Place the stems of assorted greenery in position, making sure that *there are long flowing pieces of ivy on each side of the basket and a good mass of green foliage covering the foam. Keep the foliage reasonably low and well below the handle of the basket.*

2 Add the lilies, with one in the center to give height and one trailing on each side to blend with the ivy. Remember that the lilies will be tightly shut when you arrange them, and they will open only a day or so later, so leave room for them to expand! Add the other flowers in groups, leaving room at the front for the grapes and a space at the side for the other fruit.

3 Impale each vegetable and each piece of fruit, except the grapes, on a stick. Arrange the fruit in the foam in groups. You can insert the grapes either by wrapping a strong wire around the stem and inserting it in the foam or by simply laying them in the arrangement. It is important to water the foam regularly, as there will be many stems needing to take up water if the flowers are to survive for a reasonable length of time.

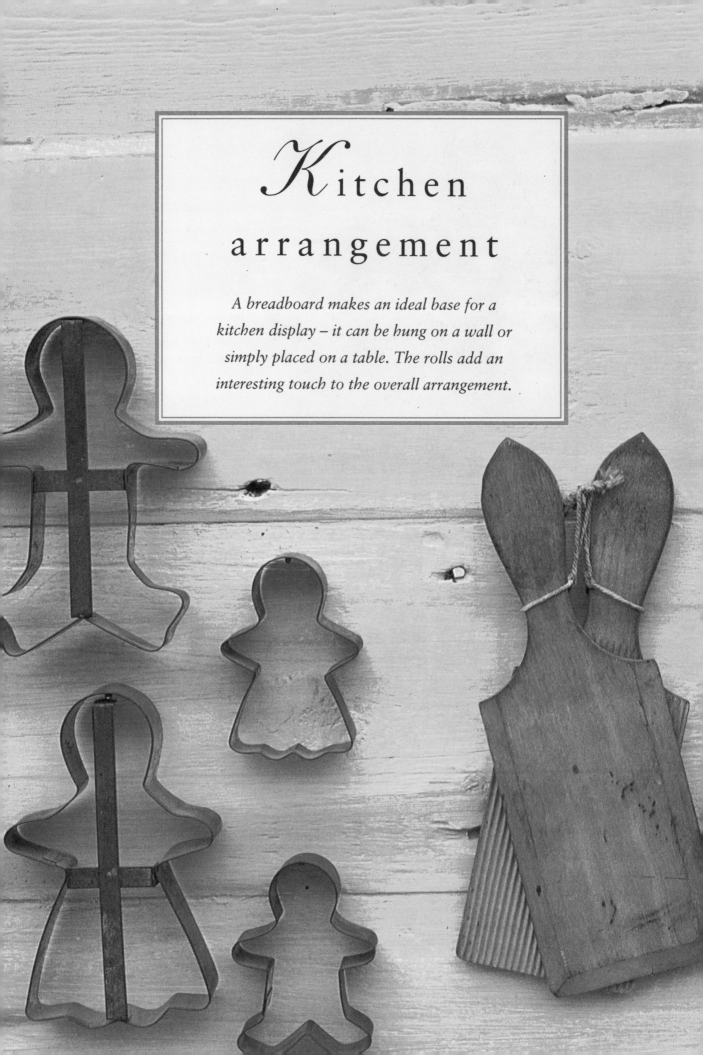

Kitchen
arrangement

A breadboard makes an ideal base for a kitchen display – it can be hung on a wall or simply placed on a table. The rolls add an interesting touch to the overall arrangement.

$\mathcal{K}$itchen arrangement

This decorated breadboard hangs above my stove and has looked very attractive for many years. It is important to give the finished arrangement a good coat of varnish, which will make it much easier to keep clean. The rolls should be dried in a slow oven and then heavily varnished. Silver-colored wire will be less conspicuous than green floral wire. You will need some marjoram, bay leaves, and wheat.

INGREDIENTS

Fine-gauge wire

Herbs and foliage, see above

A breadboard, approximately 10 inches (25 cm) in diameter, with D ring hanger

6 cinnamon sticks

Glue gun and glue

4 assorted rolls

2 terracotta ornaments or flowerpots

6 slices each of dried orange and dried green grapefruit

Wood spray varnish

1 Wire the ears of wheat into small clumps of three ears. Lay them on the board, and move them around until you are happy with their placement. Then position the cinnamon sticks so that they cover the wheat stems. Glue them down firmly.

*2 Glue on the rolls and
terracotta ornaments. If you
cannot find similar little jugs,
terracotta pots would look
fine. Glue on the marjoram to
fill any gaps.*

*3 Add the fruit slices, if
necessary cutting them in half
so that they do not protrude
too far. Then fill in any gaps
with bay leaves. Finally, give
the arrangement a good spray
of wood varnish – outside,
because of the fumes.*

Growing & drying herbs

In the Middle Ages, the mistress of the manor house had her own still room – a place where she concocted her household recipes and remedies using herbs. She would have made potpourris, healing balms, and potions to sweeten and disinfect the air. Unfortunately, these household crafts have long since been superseded by aerosols and much more potent medicine, and herbs have been relegated to the kitchen. However, the use of herbs need not be limited to flavoring food. Try incorporating them in your flower arrangements, and once you start you will be hooked – they seem to add a much more subtle dimension and interest compared with popular garden foliage.

Many herbal plants are fairly small in scale and, as such, do not mix with larger garden plants such as gladioli or enormous chrysanthemums. However, used in fair-sized bunches, as opposed to individual stems, they make a good contribution to small and medium-sized arrangements and add a lovely country simplicity as well as a traditional touch to your decorating. Country-style arrangements and traditional displays with flowers in dainty Victorian-style containers and baskets all cry out for herbs to be included. Try incorporating them into your more usual choice of greenery, and you will be pleased with the extra detail and perfume they bring to a flower display.

GROWING HERBS

You will find that herbs are a very simple group of plants to grow in the garden. Start by growing a collection of half a dozen that appeal to you the most and see how you get on. I would recommend growing one of the mints, but beware how fast they spread – they will soon take over a large area. The best way to combat this is to plant the mint in a large sheet of plastic to inhibit the amount of space it can take up.

Thyme and sage are also relatively easy to grow, and growing a bay hedge can be very useful. The bay leaves can be used in cooking but are also a very good basic foliage for many arrangements, both herbal and non-herbal. Fennel is another herb that is very simple to grow; the flowers can be used fresh or dried in arrangements and the leaves are useful in many cookery recipes. You could also try growing basil and parsley, although these may be more difficult. Basil seems to perform well for some and not for others, and likewise parsley. But give it a try, and you could be one of the lucky ones!

If you do not have room in a flowerbed outside, try growing some herbs in pots on a balcony or even indoors. I find that outdoor herbs are always healthier – those grown indoors can be subjected to too much heat or light and become pale and leggy.

DRYING HERBS

You can air-dry herbs by hanging them in small bunches, tied with rubber bands, in a warm, airy place. However, if you want a small amount of herbs for culinary use or for use in potpourri, you can also dry them in a microwave. Use a couple of sheets of paper towel as a base, and lay the herbs in small pieces on the paper. Place them in the microwave, and cook on a medium to high setting for a couple of minutes; then check to see whether they are sufficiently dry. This method does not work for herbs you want to use in an arrangement, as the drying process can make the herbs very brittle and they can be dried only in small pieces, but it can be very useful.

DISPLAYING HERBS

Air-dried bunches of herbs look very attractive hung in rows across a kitchen ceiling. Alternatively you can arrange bunches of herbs along the top of tall kitchen cabinets to achieve a similar effect. An old laundry airer suspended from the ceiling is another very effective way of displaying your harvest!

Herbs are such informal plants that dried bunches can look terrific tied with a simple ribbon or thick string and laid in fireside baskets or tra-

ditional garden baskets. Their soft colors blend well with many other dried ingredients. They look very pretty included in a romantic garland of flowers for a country-style bedroom decoration.

Dried herbs are also invaluable for scented pillows and sachets. Hops are well known for their sleep-inducing properties, but many pleasant blends of herbs can relax you and help you sleep just by giving out such a wonderful perfume. Add a soft scent to your linens by tying bunches of herbs with ribbons and suspending them from shelves or hooks in the linen closet.

Add either fresh or dried herbs to your flower arrangements for a lovely country simplicity.

CHAPTER 3

*F*lowers for Christmas

Christmas is a time not only for families and celebrations but also for flowers and decorations. Whether you are spending Christmas in a small apartment or a big family house, there is always a place to hang a decoration or two.

Homemade Christmas gifts are very precious, and special wrapping adds to the festive effect. In this chapter there are ideas for wrapping presents and for making all sorts of arrangements from holly rings to topiary trees, all of which will add extra sparkle.

Because Christmas is a time for sharing and joining in, many of these projects could by made by younger flower arrangers, but with plenty of adult supervision, of course!

So whether you are planning your floral decorations for Christmas well in advance or looking through for last-minute ideas, I hope you enjoy the projects and are inspired to move on to other creative ideas and designs.

Holly & ivy wreath

Christmas wreaths are a welcome sight on doors during the festive season. This idea is a little different, with the golden eggs adding an extra sparkle. The basic wreath can be made at home, or you can use a commercial wreath as the base.

Holly & ivy wreath

A traditional holly wreath always looks pretty at Christmas and will last well against the elements. This combination of holly and ivy will last for quite some time, and the feature of the twigs and gilded eggs adds an unusual twist to a very popular Christmas decoration. You will need plenty of sprays of holly and some very long trails of ivy. To empty the eggs of their contents, pierce them at each end with a large needle, waggling the needle inside the egg to break down the white and yolk, and then blow gently through one end. Once the eggs are empty, rinse the shells well with clean water to make sure all the contents have been removed, and leave them to drain overnight.

INGREDIENTS

Glue gun and glue

Holly and ivy, see above

A wreath base, 12 inches (30cm) in diameter

A bundle of lichen-covered twigs

5 eggs

Gold spray paint

1 Glue the sprays of holly all around the ring, covering it evenly but not so densely that you cannot see the base underneath. Both plain holly and variegated holly look very attractive, or you could use a mixture of both. If you cannot find any holly, another evergreen leaf could be substituted.

2 Wind the trails of ivy around the wreath, bending them through the holly leaves and in and out of the center of the ring. This will hold them securely enough, but you could glue each end to keep them in a particular position. Make sure the ivy has been given a long drink in water before you use it, which will help the ring stay fresh for as long as possible.

3 Glue the lichen-covered twigs in place. You could either add the twigs to a central point or offset them to one side. Spray the eggs with gold paint, and, when dry, glue them to the cluster of twigs. Place a few ivy leaves between each of the eggs to complete the festive decoration.

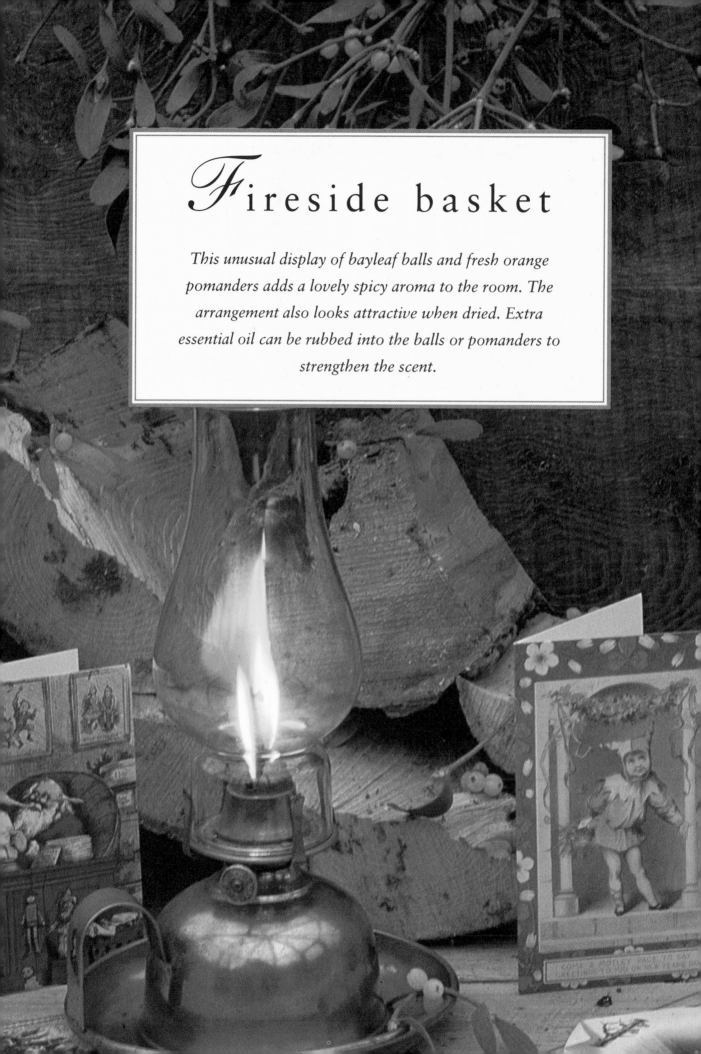

Fireside basket

This unusual display of bayleaf balls and fresh orange pomanders adds a lovely spicy aroma to the room. The arrangement also looks attractive when dried. Extra essential oil can be rubbed into the balls or pomanders to strengthen the scent.

$\mathcal{F}$ireside basket

Whether you have a real log fire or just a radiator, the warmth will help release the lovely natural perfume of these pomanders. The bay leaf balls are a little tricky to make but last well and can be enjoyed for ages after they have been made. The orange pomanders can be enjoyed while they are drying and then arranged with fruit or as a decoration on their own. You will need a shopping bag full of fresh bay leaves – more than you might think you need, as many may well be damaged. The oranges also take quite a few cloves, so it is best to buy a large pack or two from a herb supplier.

INGREDIENTS

Bay leaves

Medium–heavy gauge florist's wires

Dried-flower foam balls, about 2¼ inch (7cm) and 3¼ inch (9cm) in diameter

Glue

Cloves

Oranges

❧

1 Sort out the bay leaves, discarding any that are damaged. Cut the wire into approximately 2-inch (5cm) lengths, and bend each in half to make a "hairpin". Use these hairpins to pin the bay leaves onto each foam ball, so the entire surface is covered. The patterns you create are up to you – you can start from the top or middle, so long as the leaves overlap each time.

2 *Continue to cover the ball until the foam is completely covered. Cover the joins between the rows of leaves by changing direction and pinning leaves across each other. The last few leaves can be glued on with a small amount of glue to prevent the wires from being seen.*

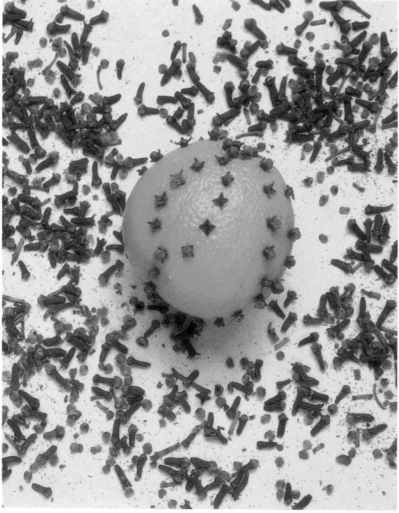

3 *Tip the cloves onto a flat surface and press them one by one into the skin of each orange. You can make many different patterns with the cloves – swirls and stripes or patches, circles, and sections. Place the decorated oranges in the basket together with the bay leaf balls.*

Christmas potpourri

Memories of Christmas are as much about scents and aromas as they are of tastes and sights. Spiced wine mulling in a large pan, aromatic cinnamon, and tangy oranges – all of these bring Christmas memories to mind. A festive potpourri can encapsulate many of these fragrances. For this recipe, you will need 10 slices of dried orange, 10 cinnamon sticks, 10 nutmegs, a cup each of dried marigold flowers, dried green leaves, rose hips, and small pine cones. For the essential oils, I used a mixture of cinnamon, ginger, and orange.

INGREDIENTS

Dried ingredients, see above

Bowl and metal spoon

½ oz (15g) orrisroot

2 tsp (10ml) essential oils of your choice

Large plastic bag and rubber band

Container for potpourri

❧

1 Assemble all the ingredients; put aside some orange slices and cinnamon sticks to decorate the top, but cut or break the rest. Place the ingredients in a bowl, add the orrisroot and essential oils, and mix well with a metal spoon.

2 Tip the mixture into a large plastic bag and shake well. Secure the top with a rubber band, and store for at least a week for the perfumes to mature and blend. Then tip the potpourri into the container, and decorate the top with the reserved orange slices and cinnamon sticks.

$\mathcal{F}$loral packages & $\mathcal{C}$hristmas crackers

Beautifully gift-wrapped parcels need not take hours to do or cost a lot. These floral giftwrap ideas are inexpensive and make a present really special. Traditional English Christmas crackers, too, can look really sumptuous with some extra decorations.

$\mathscr{F}$loral packages

Half the fun of receiving presents at Christmas is looking at them under the tree or appreciating the wrapping before you open the gift. Anticipation is certainly one of the best parts of any celebration! You can add small floral decorations very simply to Christmas and other gifts, and it makes the present mean so much more. There are three different ideas featured here, but you will be able to think of many more once you have the flowers on hand together with a box of "useful bits" that you have saved throughout the year. To make these decorations you will need 2 yellow roses, 2 sprays of carnation, a spray of golden rod, and spruce for the first design; 2 or 3 long strands of ivy for the second; and a small piece of spruce and a poinsettia flower for the third.

INGREDIENTS

Plain wrapping paper

Flowers and foliage, see above

Assorted wires

1 yard (1m) orange chiffon ribbon (1st design)

Glue

3½ yards (3m) narrow gold curling ribbon (2nd design)

½ yard (50cm) thick red and gold cord (3rd design)

❧

1 *After wrapping the present, make a small bunch with the roses and spray carnations and wrap some wire firmly around them. Add the spruce at the back of the bunch and some pieces of golden rod at the sides. Wire the whole bunch firmly. Tie the ribbon around the bunch in a pretty bow. Fix the bunch to the parcel either by gluing it down or by tying it in place with ribbons.*

2 *Wrap the present firmly, making the corners as neat as possible. Take a long strand of ivy and tie it around one* side *of the parcel. Using small strands, tie those into the first strand so that they come out at various angles. Cut the* ribbon *in half, then tie it in the middle of the ivy and curl it by winding it around a pencil.*

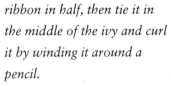

3 *Take a piece of spruce as a backing, and wire it together with a poinsettia flower. Once the wire is bound tightly around the flower, trim away any excess, and tie the piece of cord into a bow around the spray. Attach to the parcel either with a little glue or by tying it on.*

Christmas crackers

You can add a touch of Old World tradition to the Yuletide dinner table with these British Christmas party favors. Known as "crackers" – presumably from the sound produced when they are snapped open (pulled from each end by two people) – they typically contain a tissue-paper crown (which one instantly dons and wears throughout the meal), a joke, and several trinkets. Apart from their amusement value, crackers can enhance the festive look of the table, especially if you decorate them yourself. Simply wrapped crackers can be ordered from the addresses given on page 174. For the trimmings you will need some gold-sprayed foliage, cinnamon sticks, small pine cones, and dried orange slices.

INGREDIENTS

English Christmas crackers

Glue gun and glue

Foliage and spices, see above

Gold-wired cord

❧

1 Remove any commercial trimmings from the crackers, unless they blend with the decorations you are adding, like a twist of gold tinsel or something similar. Cut two or three small sprays of gold leaves and carefully glue them to the center of the cracker – use the minimum amount of glue so that it does not show.

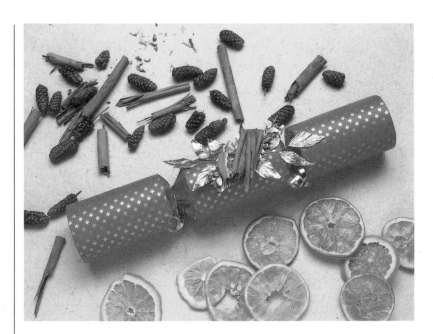

2 *Add two or three small pieces of cinnamon stick, gluing them on individually. Then place a few small pieces of orange between the cinnamon and the cracker, leaving room for the small pine cones.*

3 *Glue into place on the cracker two or three very small pine cones. Loops of gold-wired cord can be added* *to give a stylish finishing touch. You could substitute many other ingredients for the decorations, depending* *upon the scraps and trimmings you have on hand.*

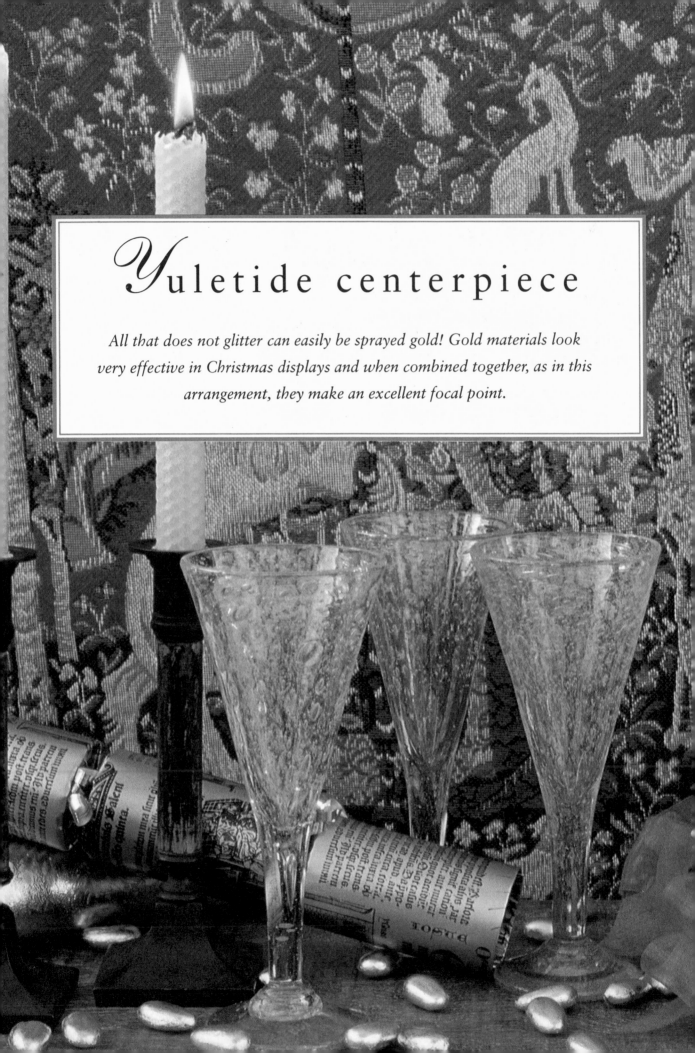

Yuletide centerpiece

All that does not glitter can easily be sprayed gold! Gold materials look very effective in Christmas displays and when combined together, as in this arrangement, they make an excellent focal point.

$\mathscr{Y}$uletide centerpiece

The main thing to aim for with a Christmas centerpiece is a bright, cheerful arrangement that will add some festive sparkle. The table is always crowded with glasses, plates, and other dishes so it is best to keep any floral decorations fairly compact. Most of the items in this arrangement have been sprayed with gold paint, which adds a special glow to the display. You will need some preserved oak foliage, 5 cardoon heads, 15 gilded pine cones, 15 natural walnuts, and 9 golden mushrooms.

INGREDIENTS

Glue

A plastic pinholder

Oval cork base, 10×8 inches (25×20cm)

Half block of dried flower foam

Pruning shears

Medium-gauge florist's wires, preferably silver

3½ yards (3m) bronze chiffon ribbon

1 Glue the pinholder to the cork base. Once it is firmly fixed in place, impale the dried flower foam over the prongs. Cover the surface of the foam with sprays of gold oak leaves, keeping the oval shape of the arrangement. If the foam seems too high, cut some off the top with a knife to make the arrangement slightly shallower.

2 *Push the gilded cardoon heads into the foam, making sure they are well spaced and not too close together. You will need very short stem lengths on these, or they will stick out too far. Wire up the pine cones by winding some wire around the base petals of the cone, then bend down the wire and use as a stem. Add them to the arrangement.*

3 *Fill in the arrangement with wired walnuts (if you prefer you could glue them in place) and wired golden mushrooms. Take some* chiffon ribbon and make a few loops, holding the base of the loops between your thumb and forefinger. Then wrap wire around the base to secure (see diagram on page 131), bend down the wire, and push it into the arrangement. Place loops on both sides of the centerpiece.

Traditional arrangement

This very traditional combination of poinsettias, holly, and conifer sprigs always looks attractive at Christmas time. If you prefer a larger version, the poinsettias could be used in their pots rather than in foam.

$\mathcal{T}$raditional arrangement

Although it is fun to make modern or unusual flower arrangements and come up with new ideas as often as possible, it is also very satisfying to make a really traditional Christmas arrangement. This particular idea reminds me of many Christmas cards I have received over the years, and I like the comforting feel of an arrangement one almost seems to recognize! For the foliage, I used a mixture of blue spruce and variegated holly, about 9 stems of each, and 3 large red poinsettia flowers.

INGREDIENTS

Long shallow container, approximately 8 × 4 inches (20 × 10cm)

Fresh flower foam to fit container

3 candle holders

3 ivory candles

Foliage and flowers, see above

2 yards (2m) red ribbon, 1 inch (2.5cm) wide

2 × medium–heavy gauge florist's wires

1 Soak the foam in water until it is saturated. Wedge the foam into the container. Press the three candle holders into the foam wherever you would like them. Trim two of the candles so that they are differing heights. Fix the candles into the candle holders. Place 6-inch (15cm) long sprays of both kinds of foliage in the arrangement.

2 *Cut the poinsettia stems to a suitable length, and add them to the arrangement. Keep them spaced well apart so that they do not look too crowded.*

3 *Make two wired bows from the ribbon (see page 131), and place them on each side of the arrangement so that the display can be viewed from both sides. Take care never to leave the arrangement unattended when the candles are alight, as indoor bonfires are most unwelcome!*

Topiary tree & Indoor wreath

The little apple and cranberry topiary tree is a pretty and unusual decoration which is simple enough for children to make. The wreath is an idea for indoors, as the ingredients are definitely not weather-proof.

Topiary tree

There are many differing designs for topiary trees, but this one uses the unusual combination of fruit and foliage instead of flowers. Because most of the ingredients are dried, it should last well; the cranberries will shrivel or go moldy after a while, but they can be replaced by fresh or artificial berries. The clear glass container makes a change from a terracotta base, but a basket or pot could be used if you prefer. You will need about 60 apple slices to include in the base, a pack of fresh cranberries, a bunch of preserved beech leaves, and some hazelnuts.

INGREDIENTS

Piece of dried flower foam

Sharp knife

Glass base, approximately 5 inches (12cm) square

Fruit and foliage, see above

Thick cinnamon stick for trunk

2¾-inch (7cm) dried flower foam ball

Assorted wires

1 Cut the foam to size with a sharp knife, leaving room for the apple slices, and insert in the glass base. Camouflage the foam on all sides with apple slices; arrange them so that they overlap or touch. Choose a fairly thick cinnamon stick, about 8–9 inches (20–23cm) long, and push this into the center of the foam.

2 *Cover the surface of the base with hazelnuts. Impale the foam ball onto the cinnamon stick and cover it with sprays of beech leaves. If necessary, wire together bunches of individual leaves if the ends of the sprays are not bushy enough.*

3 *Wire the apple slices individually, and then push the ends of the wires into the foam tree, placing them evenly among the beech foliage throughout the arrangement. Cut shorter pieces of wire for the cranberries. Insert one end of the wire into a cranberry and the other into the tree. As before, dot the cranberries among the foliage. Finally, sprinkle some cranberries among the hazelnuts at the base of the tree for extra color.*

$\mathcal{I}$ndoor wreath

Many people have a welcoming wreath on their front door at Christmas. This design is intended for indoor use, as the dried flowers simply would not survive the elements. It could be hung in a hallway or on an inside door, depending on where you have a space. Again, some of the ingredients have been sprayed gold, and it is interesting to see how well they blend with the naturally colored material. To make this indoor wreath, you will need a bunch of eucalyptus and some blue spruce, a bunch of gilded poppy heads, a bunch of preserved and gilded foliage, such as boxwood, and 20 pink roses.

INGREDIENTS

Wreath base, 12 inches (30cm) in diameter

Flowers and foliage, see above

Glue

1⅝ yards (1·5m) wired ribbon, 3 inches (8cm) wide

Assorted wires

❧

1 Cover the base roughly with blue spruce, and glue this firmly in place. Add pieces of eucalyptus to thicken up the background. Make a bow with the ribbon (see page 131).

118

2 Glue the bow onto the ring. Add in the gilded poppy heads and box, curving the ingredients around with the circle, covering about three-quarters of the wreath.

3 Finally, glue the pink roses onto the ring. These are best placed in groups of three or five, in between the gilded poppy heads and box foliage. This design would look equally pretty if the poppies and box were sprayed silver instead of gold.

Festive garland

This luxurious spruce garland can be made at home
for a fairly reasonable price. Although it takes a little
while to make, it does look wonderful!

$\mathcal{F}$estive garland

Spruce is a very attractive foliage to use at Christmas, and it has the added benefit of lasting very well. It will not drop like some conifers or traditional Christmas trees – it just dries and turns a grayish-blue instead of bluish-green. It will take a reasonable amount of spruce to make this garland – about 50 sprigs to make a 1½-yard (1.4m) garland. It is hard to be accurate about the exact number required, as it depends on the quality and density of the spruce.

INGREDIENTS

2 yards (1·8m) twisted paper ribbon

Medium-gauge floral wire

Spruce, see above

1 yard (1m) wired ribbon, 2½–3 inches (7–8cm) wide

Glue gun and glue

Assortment of gilded poppy heads, cinnamon sticks, walnuts, dried orange slices, pine cones, and gilded lotus heads

Spray gloss varnish
ð

1 Bend some twisted paper ribbon over at both ends, and wire firmly to make a hanging loop at each end of the garland. Twist a small piece of wire in the middle of the garland to remind you where the center is. Starting from one end, place a 4-inch (10cm) sprig of spruce over the loop and wire it onto the twisted paper ribbon. Keep adding pieces of spruce, fanning them out so the garland is fairly flat rather than thick. Continue until you reach the marked middle point, then turn the garland around and start from the other end.

2 *Once you reach the middle point, cut some smaller pieces of spruce, place them at right angles to the ribbon, and wire on to fill the gap in the middle. Use plenty of wire, as it is more important to have a secure garland than a neat one, and the glued-on bits will cover most wiring problems. Make a large bow with the ribbon (see page 131) and attach it to the center with glue.*

3 *Glue on all the decorations you have chosen. Position larger pieces like the lotus heads first, and the cinnamon sticks through the center of* *the bow and at intervals along the garland. Once you have all your nuts and cones glued on, give them a coat of spray gloss varnish, as this* *will highlight their colors and give the nuts, in particular, an attractive shine.*

Christmas tree decorations

We all have many beloved family tree decorations that have been around for years – some may be very special as they were made by the children. Although there are always new, different, and exciting commercially made tree decorations on the market, these homemade decorations are a little bit different, and something perhaps the whole family could make together a couple of days before Christmas. You will need some sea lavender, golden rod, spray carnation, 1 or 2 roses, and any fresh foliage from the garden.

INGREDIENTS

Gold wire or cord

Terracotta flowerpots, 1 inch (2.5cm) in diameter

Green floral foam

Flowers and foliage, see above

Fine-gauge floral wire

Cellophane

Narrow curling ribbon

🎗

1 Thread two loops of gold wire or cord through the hole in the base of each flowerpot to act as hanging loops for the decoration. Fill the pots with foam that has first been soaked in water, and make a miniature arrangement with foliage, sea lavender, and golden rod. The ingredients can be altered according to what is available.

2 Take some carnations or roses with sea lavender or golden rod, and wire into a small bunch. Add a wrapping of cellophane and secure it with the ribbon, adding a loop to hang them from the tree.

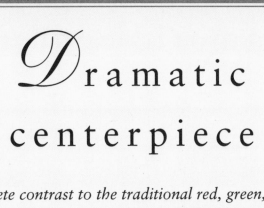

$\mathcal{D}$ramatic centerpiece

*In complete contrast to the traditional red, green, and gold
Christmas color schemes, these orchids look absolutely
stunning in this unusual centerpiece. The twigs
can be found lying on the ground in woods and fields.*

Dramatic centerpiece

The coloring of this arrangement is by no means traditional, but it is certainly dramatic and would be ideal for a New Year's Eve celebration. Although it looks very impressive, the actual arrangement is very easy and will take only a short while to make. The list of materials is quite short – you will need 2 small bunches of mauve Singapore orchids, a selection of lichen-covered twigs, and some hellebore leaves.

INGREDIENTS

Fresh flower foam

Small ring mold or other container, approximately 6 inches (15cm) wide

Flowers and twigs, see above

ॐ

1 *Soak the foam in water until it is saturated, and fill the mold with it. Lay the twigs in position if you are arranging the flowers in situ; if not, lay them on the table and add the container with flowers after Step 3.*

2 *Insert the hellebore leaves into the foam, making the arrangement long or round, depending on the shape of your table. If you cannot obtain hellebore leaves, any other large, dark leaves would be suitable.*

3 *Next add the sprays of Singapore orchids. If they are very long, break them in half and add both halves toward* *the center of the display. These orchids are also available in other colors, so the arrangement could be* *varied simply by the substitution of cream or peach orchids, for example.*

$\mathcal{P}$reparing for Christmas

Many of the items used in these projects can be bought all year round, but some may need a little advance preparation. Think ahead during the summer days; harvest flowers and seed heads for drying at the right time, and store them away in a warm, dark place.

PLANNING AHEAD

The projects using dried or preserved items can be made in advance and stored. Make sure, however, that you pack them away carefully – preferably in the dark. It is all too easy for another member of the family to damage something that has been carelessly left in the spare room.

Fresh ingredients such as blue spruce and holly can be cut a little while before Christmas, but make sure they are kept cool and damp. If you live in a rainy climate, spruce lasts very well out-of-doors, where it can benefit from showers.

SPRAYING WITH GOLD AND SILVER PAINT

Spraying plant material, such as dried seed heads, with gold or silver paint can add a truly festive touch to arrangements. There is no need to stop at seed pods or other dried flower parts when you are thinking of things to spray. Artificial fruit looks wonderful with a coat of gold or silver – and that includes the cheapest, most unrealistic plastic specimens which you never thought would be useful at all. Bargain baskets and containers that were a hideous color look quite transformed when they are given a liberal coating of gold or copper metallic spray.

Spraying with gold paint can be a very messy affair. The easiest way is to lay the items you want to spray in a large shallow fruit box – the kind used by supermarkets. Spray one side, and then once they have dried off a little, turn them over and spray the other. If you decide to take items out in the garden to spray, take care to protect your hands and shoes. The spray drifts quite a lot, and I have ruined a couple of pairs of shoes with the addition of gold paint speckles!

MAKING A WREATH BASE

As a change from using store-bought wreath bases, you might consider making your own wreaths or rings. You could try using lengths of vine or clematis stems, but for a really sturdy wreath I have found the trimmings from a willow tree the most successful material.

Place some nails in a board in the pattern shown in the diagram opposite. The size of the board will depend on the desired finished size of the wreath. Wind the stems in and out of the nails on the board, making a good circular shape, easing each piece around the bends. Continue with plenty of stems until you have a sturdy wreath. As the depth of the ring increases, try to wind some of the stems through the others to make the wreath even more secure. Once you feel that you have a wreath of the shape and size that you are happy with, slide some pieces of wire under the ring in various places around the circle, and knot or twist the wire so that it holds the depth of the ring in shape.

Leave your wreath on the board to dry in a warm place until the stems have dried completely. This will take varying amounts of time, depending on the variety of plant material used and the moisture in it.

MAKING A BOW

Bows always feature prominently in Christmas arrangements and wrappings. Making a wired bow is much easier than it looks and is a technique worth trying. The diagram on the right illustrates where the wire should be tied. Take a length of ribbon and wrap it around like wrapping a shawl around your shoulders. Gather up the middle, making a bow and tails, and bind the middle with some wire. The wire can be hidden with a small piece of ribbon with flowers, or other decorations. Another method of making a bow is shown below.

The overall effect at Christmas should be one of abundance and cheerfulness. So don't worry too much about the technical side of your ideas or arrangements, just have fun, rope as many of the family in as possible, and make the house look happy and friendly.

Collect an assortment of useful Christmas decorations for your arrangements (above). Make a wired bow in two ways, and a board for a wreath base (below).

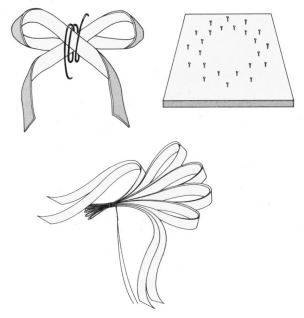

CHAPTER 4

*F*loral Gifts

Flowers make wonderful gifts for all age groups, and for both sexes. Although traditionally flowers have been given as gifts to women, there are many male gardeners who would love to receive a gift of plants or a bunch of flowers.

A gift made with dried flowers has the bonus of early preparation – you can make Christmas or birthday offerings well in advance, provided that they are kept fairly warm and dark to prevent any absorption of moisture or color loss. If you plan to make quite a number of your own Christmas presents, any that can be made and tucked away are an invaluable help to finishing everything on time! Although some of the projects are aimed for specific occasions, they can easily be adapted, with a small change here and there, to suit many others. If you have a good collection of basic flower-arranging items such as foam, containers, wires, and ribbons, you can make a present very quickly should the need arise.

Centerpiece

A combination of fresh and preserved material gives this centerpiece an unusual look, which can be changed very easily by adding new fresh flowers to the small displays on each side of the basket. The center can be filled with chocolates, nuts, or fruit.

Centerpiece

This arrangement is a useful way of combining a gift of chocolates and flowers, or you can use it to decorate a table and hold after-dinner chocolates. The rim of the basket is decorated mainly with dried flowers and so can be used over and over again, whereas the small arrangements at each side use fresh flowers which can easily be replaced for each occasion. The chocolates will unfortunately have to be replaced regularly as they are bound to be eaten rather rapidly! You will need some glycerined copper beech or other preserved foliage and a selection of nuts, dried apple slices, canella berries, pine cones, and a bunch of pink alstroemeria, 10 roses and about 15 large ivy leaves.

INGREDIENTS

Two small containers

Green floral foam

A shallow basket, approximately 12 inches (30cm) in diameter

Glue gun and glue

Flowers, foliage, fruit, and nuts, see above

Spray gloss varnish

Chocolates or other candies

❧

1 *Fill the small containers (I used cut-down aerosol can tops) with floral foam, and soak it well. Attach the containers to the basket.*

Using a hot glue gun, attach the dried foliage around the rim of the basket so that it is evenly decorated and the containers are camouflaged.

136

2 *Glue the selection of fruit and nuts to each side of the basket, filling the sides well to look abundant and interesting. Any nuts are suitable, but chestnuts are particularly effective, as are hazelnuts, pecans, and walnuts. Once you have filled the edges of the basket, give the ingredients a spray with gloss varnish; this highlights the colors and adds an attractive shine.*

3 *Arrange some ivy leaves in the green foam, and add the alstroemeria flowers, using a very short stem. Finally add in the roses, again on a very short stem. Make sure that all the flowers have been standing in deep water for some time before placing them in the arrangement. Finally fill the basket with heaps of chocolates.*

𝒫hoto frame & 𝒟ressing table nosegay

A photo frame is always a popular gift, and the addition of a small flower decoration makes this frame even more attractive. The nosegay would look charming in any bedroom, whether the lady in question is nine or ninety!

$\mathscr{P}$hoto frame

A plain photograph frame can be enlivened by the addition of a small flower arrangement and the flowers changed time and time again. The small container used in this example was a brown aerosol can lid but any other small and moderately inconspicuous container would be suitable. If the item you wish to use is a lighter color than the frame then I would suggest painting it black or dark brown to help conceal its presence. You will need only a small amount of flowers and foliage – if you do not have a garden, small pieces of houseplant foliage would be a possibility. This example uses a few hellebore leaves, three pieces of conifer, a few strands of ivy, some larger ivy leaves, and a spray of Singapore orchids.

INGREDIENTS

Small piece of green floral foam

1 dark-colored plastic container

Glue

Plain, wide photograph frame, 10 × 8 inches (25 × 20cm)

Flowers and foliage, see above

ও

1 Soak the green foam in water. Fill the container with foam, and, using a strong glue such as a hot glue gun, attach the container, foam upwards, to the bottom of the frame. Leave until completely dry.

140

2 *Arrange the pieces of foliage in the foam, covering both the foam and plastic container as much as possible. Place some taller pieces of ivy so that they come up the frame and let others trail to soften the arrangement. Any combination of greenery could be used.*

3 *Cut the spray of orchids into 2 or 3 pieces, and add them to the arrangement. Make sure the foam is kept wet but not overwatered, or it might leak onto the surface on which it is standing.*

*D*ressing table nosegay

Although bouquets are most often thought of in connection with weddings and other celebrations, they are also very pretty ornaments to have displayed around the house. This pink and cream nosegay would look charming on a dressing table. It uses a commercial bouquet holder with a foam base center. If you are unable to find one, you could achieve a similar effect by wiring all the ingredients together. To make this nosegay, you will need a small bunch of eucalyptus (fairly small-leafed variety), a bunch of dark pink larkspur, a bunch of dark pink roses, and about 20 wired cream strawflowers.

INGREDIENTS

A bouquet holder

A frill to fit the holder

Glue

Flowers and foliage, see above

1 Attach the frill to the bouquet holder with glue. Break down the eucalyptus into pieces of a suitable size. Arrange them evenly across *the foam ball in the center of the holder. Use as much eucalyptus as necessary to give a good covering to act as a base for the arrangement.*

142

2 *Cut the pink larkspur into small pieces and push them into the foam so that they are evenly spaced throughout the arrangement. Do not make them too long, or the nosegay will look straggly and untidy. Make sure the lace frill is still clearly visible.*

3 *Cut the rose stems and strawflower wires to the correct length, and place the flowers in the nosegay.*

Scatter them evenly throughout the arrangement. You should plan where they will go before inserting them

in the foam to make sure that there are not too many cream or pink flowers in any one part of the nosegay.

143

"Get well soon" basket

Nothing lifts a patient's spirits more than beautiful fresh flowers at the bedside. These fresh colors are a cheerful reminder of spring, but an equally beautiful arrangement can be made at other times of the year using different flowers.

"Get well soon" basket

If you are feeling at a low ebb, recovering from an illness or just a bad cold, nothing lifts the spirits more than some pretty fresh flowers to brighten the room. Spring flowers are particularly cheering, and lightly scented flowers help to perfume a bedroom or hospital ward but all flowers have a special magic! Avoid making the arrangement too large, as space may be at a premium, and make sure that it is easy to water and keep fresh. You will need a bunch of mimosa, a bunch of daffodils, and some greenery.

INGREDIENTS

A small basket, approximately 8×6 inches (20×15cm)

Plastic bag

Piece of green floral foam to fit basket

Flowers and foliage, see above

Scissors

Skewer or chopstick

1 Line the basket with a plastic bag (unpunctured) or some plastic sheeting. Soak the foam well in water. Wedge the foam into the basket, so that it is held in place. Using a selection of greenery, place some sprigs all the way around the basket and across the top so that the foam is completely covered.

2 *Cut the mimosa into small sprigs about ½ inch (1.2cm) longer than the greenery, and place them in the arrangement. Any light, fluffy plant material, such as baby's breath, could be substituted for the mimosa.*

3 *To place the daffodils in the arrangement, cut each one as you come to it, allowing about 1 inch (2.5cm) to go* *into the foam. Daffodil stalks do not respond well to being pushed into foam, so make a hole first with a skewer or* *chopstick and then place the daffodil in the hole.*

147

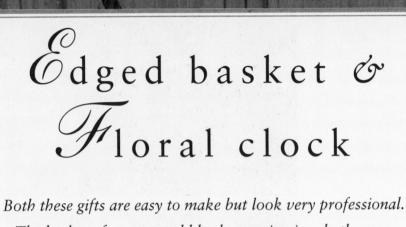

Edged basket & Floral clock

Both these gifts are easy to make but look very professional.
The basket of soaps would look stunning in a bathroom,
while the pressed flower clock adds a pretty country touch to
a kitchen or bedroom.

$\mathcal{E}$dged basket

This edged basket would make a wonderful bathroom or powder room decoration; as an alternative to putting soaps in the center you could fill it with potpourri. Or, if you wanted to give the basket as a hostess gift, you could fill it with chocolates. You will need a hot glue gun, which is much easier than trying to wire the ingredients onto the basket. This basket used some Spanish moss, 15 sticks of cinnamon, 25 nutmegs, 25 slices of dried orange, half a bunch of love-in-a-mist seed pods, and 2 bunches of Evelien roses.

INGREDIENTS

Flowers, foliage, fruit, and spices, see above

Glue gun and glue

A shallow basket with no handle, approximately 9–10 inches (23–25cm) in diameter

Fine-gauge floral wire

Scissors

Tissue paper or paper doily

Contents for basket

1 Form the Spanish moss into a sausage shape. Put some glue around the top edge of the basket, and place the moss sausage over the glue. Press down, taking care not to burn yourself. Once the glue has cooled, use some wire to bind the moss onto the basket in a few strategic points to tame it and make the moss a similar height all around the basket. Glue on the cinnamon sticks in threes.

2 Glue the nutmegs onto the piles of cinnamon, then add the orange slices, some whole and some in halves and quarters. Other citrus fruits, such as grapefruit or lemons, or some dried apple could be used. Then cut the pods from the love-in-a-mist and glue them to the basket between the bundles of cinnamon.

3 Cut the roses quite short and glue them to the basket between the love-in-a-mist seed pods. Line the basket with a little tissue paper or a paper doily, and then fill the basket with pretty guest soaps, pot pourri, chocolates, or other candies.

$\mathcal{F}$loral clock

Using pressed flowers to decorate a clock makes your gift a little more personal. But before you buy your clock, check with the store that the clock can be taken apart or it could be disastrous! You will need a selection of pressed flowers and leaves in complementary colors and of a similar size. I have used ballerina roses, pink larkspur, and rue leaves with some small pieces of yellow golden rod flowers.

INGREDIENTS

Clock with removable
glass

Pressed flowers and leaves,
see above

Tweezers

Tapestry needle

Latex adhesive

1 *Play around with the leaves and flowers at first to see what type of design you would like to do. Use tweezers so as not to damage the plant material. Once you* are happy with your ideas, you can start to glue down the design. Begin with the leaves, as they form the base of the design.*

2 *Using the tapestry needle, apply a small dab of latex adhesive to each leaf. Do not put too much on at once, or it may seep out. Here the leaves have been glued on in a circular design. Next add small pieces of golden rod between each leaf.*

3 *Make sure each flower is well glued before proceeding with the next ingredient. Lastly add the roses and the* pink larkspur. *If you have put too much adhesive behind the flowers, carefully clean it off the clock face.* *Then polish the glass and re-assemble the clock.*

Potpourri

Homemade potpourri is far superior to the mass-produced, scented wood-shaving collections usually found in shops. You can grow or harvest all manner of natural plants and pods for your mixtures, and long-lasting fragrances can be achieved using essential oils and orrisroot.

$\mathscr{P}$otpourri

This selection of four different potpourris representing the four seasons would make a wonderfully different gift at a very reasonable cost. Drying flowers and leaves for potpourri can easily be done in a microwave by laying the items on paper towels and cooking for a couple of minutes on medium to high heat. Although you lose some of the shape, the color remains, together with any fragrance. You will need four differing sets of ingredients – *Spring*: 10 lemon slices, 1 cup dried green hellebores, 1 cup dried delphinium flowers, and 1 cup any dried gray-green leaves; *Summer*: 1 cup dark pink larkspur flowers, 1½ cups ivy leaves, ½ cup cloves, and 1 cup pink rose petals plus a few whole roses; *Autumn*: 10 dried apple slices, 10 dried orange slices, 1 cup tangerine-colored rose petals, and 1 cup mixed beechnuts and peach stones; *Winter*: 1 cup conifer leaves, 1 cup small pine cones, 1 cup broken cinnamon, 1 cup red rose petals, and a few whole roses.

INGREDIENTS

Potpourri ingredients, see above

4 mixing bowls

1 ounce (30g) orrisroot

4 × small (2·5ml) bottles of essential or perfume oils

Metal spoon

4 plastic bags

4 rubber bands

4 suitable containers

Glue gun and glue

æ

1 Organize all your ingredients, making sure you have enough to fill the four containers you have chosen. Mix the four ingredients for each season together in small bowls, and add a quarter of the orrisroot to each one. Add the oil of your choice and mix well, using a metal spoon. Choose oils that reflect the ingredients used in the potpourri – for example, lemon oil for spring and cinnamon for winter.

2 *Tip the mixture for each potpourri into a separate plastic bag and shake well. Secure the tops with rubber bands and leave to mature for at least a week. The potpourri mixtures can then be emptied into their respective containers.*

3 *These plain containers are ideal for potpourri. They are inexpensive and easy to decorate for a gift. Remove* *some of the larger pieces from each potpourri, and arrange them in a pretty group on the corresponding lid. A glue gun* *is a quick and efficient way to fix them in place, but other strong glues could be used instead.*

Birthday sampler & Mother's Day basket

These delightful presents would be suitable for many occasions, other than those suggested. The striped design of the basket has a fresh, modern look, while the flower sampler is reminiscent of times gone by.

$\mathcal{B}$irthday sampler

This flower picture is intended to make one think of Victorian needlework and children's samplers. The time needed to make those beautiful works of art is quite astonishing; the pressed flower version, although still a finicky project, takes considerably less time and a little less patience. Alternative background materials, such as linen or canvas, could be used, depending upon your particular taste. The pressed flowers needed for this project are 3 ivy leaves, 7 small fern leaves, 5 pieces of sweet alyssum, 7 sprays of freesia, 3 pieces of alchemilla (lady's mantle), and a selection of pansies, roses, potentillas, and astrantias. Finally, you will also need a large number of potentilla centers – about 12 per letter.

INGREDIENTS

Wooden frame, approximately 12 × 10 inches (30 × 25 cm), with a glass and hardboard back

Piece of ⅛ inch (3mm) thick foam, approximately 12 × 10 inches (30 × 25 cm)

Piece of unbleached muslin, approximately 12 × 10 inches (30 × 25 cm)

Tweezers

Fabric glue

Flowers and foliage, see above

Large tapestry needle

🌿

1 Place the back of the frame on the table and cover it with the piece of foam. Lay the muslin on top of the foam. Using tweezers to lift the flowers, here potentilla centers, arrange the layout of the chosen name, placing it either diagonally across the picture or *horizontally across the middle. Once you are satisfied with the position of the name and shape of the letters, glue down the potentilla centers. Hold each flower with tweezers, then apply a dab of glue with a tapestry needle.*

2 *Arrange the plant material in the bottom corner of the picture, placing the ivy leaves first and then adding the freesia sprays between the leaves. Place the pale alyssum against the dark ivy leaves for contrast. Add the larger flowers next, and then the smaller ones such as the potentilla.*

3 *Then arrange the top corner of the sampler, again starting with the leaves to obtain the right shape. Place the smaller bits of alchemilla between the ferns. Then mix the pansies and roses together in the center of the design. Finally glue all the flowers firmly in place, applying the glue with the needle, and frame the picture.*

161

$\mathscr{M}$other's Day basket

Although this flower basket is very different from the style of flower arranging we are all used to, its graphic design, with stripes crossing the basket, is fun to experiment with. You can easily vary the stripes by changing the color of the contents or shape of the basket. You will need 4 or 5 hydrangea heads, 30 wired cream strawflowers, 24 heads of cream carthamus, a bunch of pink larkspur, and 8 pink peonies.

INGREDIENTS

Long, shallow basket

3 blocks of dried flower foam

Flowers, see above

🌿

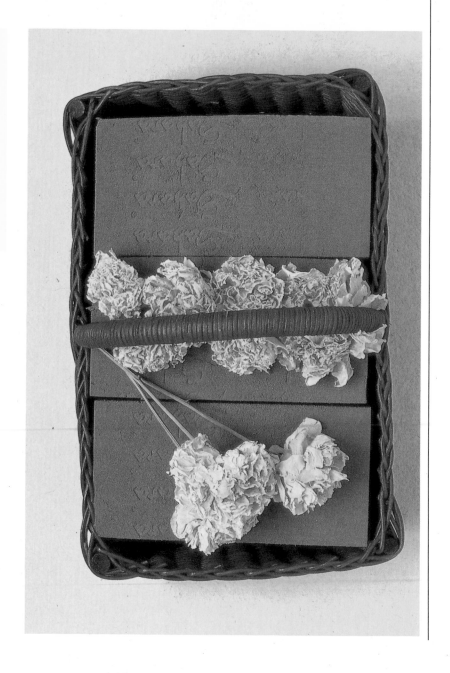

1 Fill the basket with the dried flower foam, and wedge the last piece in to make sure the foam does not move. Start the arrangement with the peonies, placing a straight row beneath the handle in the center of the basket. You will need to have very short stems on all the ingredients.

3 Complete the remaining side of the basket like the first, with bands of larkspur, carthamus, strawflowers, and finally hydrangea. Insert these so that they overlap the basket slightly to soften the edges.

2 You can either build up the stripes in the arrangement from the center outward, working on both sides at once, or complete one side of the basket at a time. Move on to the next ingredient, the larkspur. Break the bunch into short pieces about 3–4 inches (8–10cm) long. Place a band of these next to the peonies. Then put 12 heads of carthamus next to the larkspur. Next make a row of 15 strawflowers, and follow this with a final strip made from pieces of hydrangea.

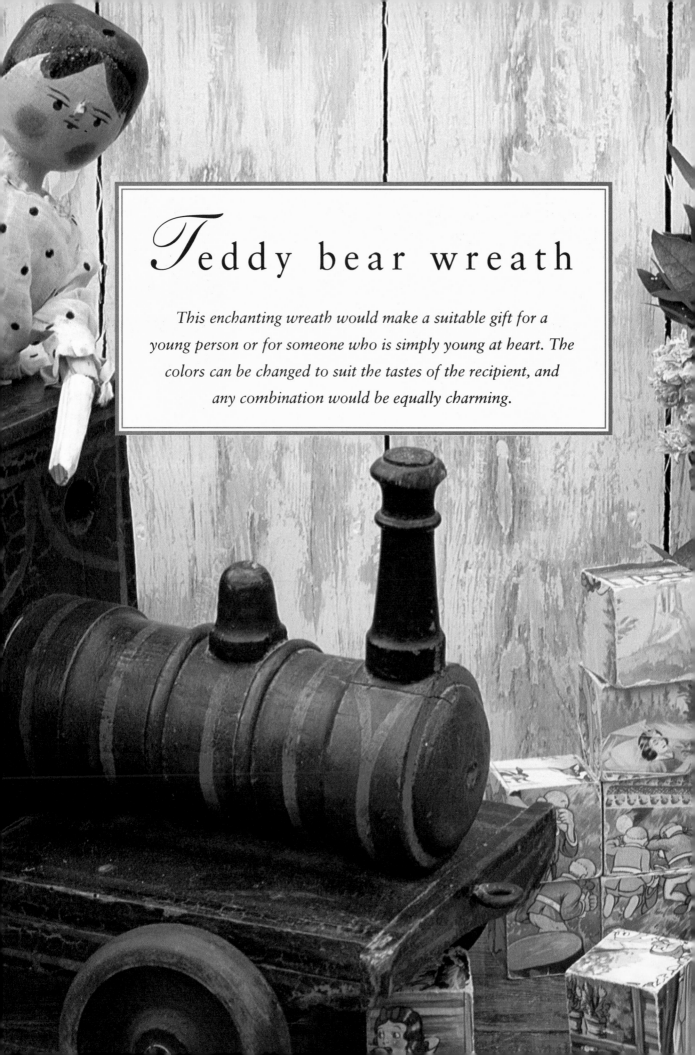

Teddy bear wreath

This enchanting wreath would make a suitable gift for a young person or for someone who is simply young at heart. The colors can be changed to suit the tastes of the recipient, and any combination would be equally charming.

*T*eddy bear wreath

This lovely little teddy bear wreath would make a special gift for the little girl in your life, or possibly for some bigger girls as well! Teddies are a perennial favorite, and although flock-covered bears have been used here, a small fluffy bear would also look adorable. You could make this wreath with fresh flowers, but it would not last long; this combination of dried and preserved materials will last well if hung away from strong light. To make the wreath, you will need a bunch of pale pink larkspur, some sprays of canella berries, half a bunch of green carthamus and some preserved foliage.

INGREDIENTS

Scissors

Flowers and foliage, see above

Glue gun and glue

Wreath base, approximately 8 inches (20cm) in diameter

Mother bear and two baby bears

1 Trim the foliage into small sprigs and glue it around the wreath. Arrange the sprigs so that some leaves face into the center of the wreath and others outward. Next, glue some preserved foliage around the wreath.

2 *Glue the teddy bears firmly in place, and hold them there until the glue has cooled completely. Add in the heads from the bunch of carthamus. This is a very versatile dried ingredient, as it has a good shape and fills arrangements well.*

3 *Now break the pink larkspur into small pieces and* *attach them around the whole wreath. Finally, fill any gaps* *with some small sprays of the canella berries.*

Wedding spoon

Spoons have been considered tokens of love and luck for many generations. A decorated wooden spoon makes an attractive good luck token for a bride. Alternatively, by using fewer flowers and including spices and fruit, you could make a suitable spoon for a kitchen.

Wedding spoon

Wooden spoons, such as the beautifully carved Welsh love spoons, are a traditional gift for a bride in many parts of Europe. Decorating a spoon with flowers is quicker and easier than carving one and is a lovely way to show your affection and wish good luck to the recipient. Although these floral spoons were designed primarily as a bridal gift, they could also make a lovely birthday or Mother's Day present or good luck gift. To make a similar wedding spoon, you will need a few flowers and pieces of foliage – flowers from the garden would be fine, or use a few leftovers from an arrangement.

INGREDIENTS

Drill

Large wooden spoon

Approximately 2¼ yards (2m) ribbon, depending upon desired length

Glue

Small green pinholder (attachment for use with floral foam)

Scissors

Tiny cube of green floral foam

Flowers and foliage, see above

&

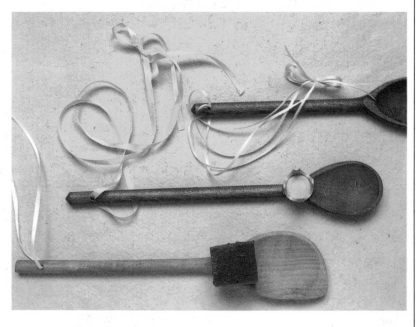

1 Drill a hole in the top of the handle of the spoon, either from front to back or from side to side, making sure it is large enough to take your choice of ribbon. Thread the ribbon through the hole and tie it into a firm bow. Glue the pinholder to the junction of the handle and the bowl of the spoon. Trim the prongs of the pinholder to make it a little smaller. Impale a cube of foam, soaked in water, onto the pinholder.

2 *Cover the foam well with some pieces of greenery; unusual elements such as catkins look lovely. Allow the foliage to trail over the spoon handle and bowl in a random fashion.*

3 *Add in some flowers. You will need to trim the stems to about 2–3 inches (5–8cm). Here I've used a small number of spray carnations. Try to choose flowers that last fairly well out of water. Wildflowers never last well and look much nicer left in the country, but many garden flowers would be suitable.*

Preparing flowers for gifts

Packaging is a very important part of making your own gifts. A pretty box or ribbon, some cellophane or a special container can raise a homemade display into a special handmade creation! If you spend a little extra time planning the presentation of your gift, your efforts will be amply rewarded by the appreciative comments when you hand over the present.

Collecting various items in advance is well worth doing. I have a deep drawer that is full of odds and ends that may well be just what I'm looking for – one day! Seriously, though, a collection of boxes, ribbons, pretty paper and string, and other trimmings can make present manufacturing much easier.

CARE OF FRESH FLOWERS

If you are planning to give a gift of fresh flowers, it is obviously important to have the best quality flowers, which have been treated to last as long as possible. If you grow flowers for cutting in your garden, these should be fresh and with proper conditioning should last well. Good-quality flowers from a florist can last even longer, as they are often grown to be long lasting. It is important to have a good source for your flowers as half-dead flowers will never make a good arrangement, and your time will not have been used to its best advantage.

Once you get your flowers indoors, whether they are home-grown or from a florist, cut the bottom of the stalks at an angle and immerse the flowers in deep water overnight. This will give them a good long drink, which should help them to last longer in your arrangements.

DRYING FLOWERS

Many flowers will dry just as well at home as in commercial drying kilns. Producing an arrangement that you have grown and dried yourself is very satisfying.

Collect the flowers you wish to dry on a bright, dry day, and harvest them just before they reach their full maturity. Strip off some of the lower leaves, and tie them in small bunches, fixing them with a strong rubber band. It is important not to use string for this purpose, for the stems shrink during the drying process, and the bunch might fall and damage some of your precious blooms!

Hang these small bunches somewhere warm and dark, but with reasonable air circulation. A dry loft or attic can be ideal – a garage is not suitable as the night temperatures might be too low to be beneficial to the flowers. A spare bedroom or closet with the doors ajar can sometimes be a solution. Once the flowers are dry, they can be stored in boxes packed with tissue paper and kept at a reasonable temperature.

PRESSING FLOWERS

Preserving flowers in a press is an easy technique if all the basic pointers are followed. Many people use presses (often unsuccessfully) as children, but good pressing is possible only if a few basic rules are followed.

• Collect only perfect specimens that have begun to open that day – and pick only on a bright, dry day, preferably in the morning.

• Choose mainly thin or flat flowers, such as pansies, larkspur, and small daisies, and avoid thick, lumpy specimens such as chrysanthemums and thick-centered daisies.

• Use clean, dry blotting paper and pads of dry newspaper in your press. Place a pad of newspaper at the bottom of the press and cover it with a sheet of blotting paper. Lay a few flowers on the blotting paper, making sure they do not touch or overlap, and then cover them with more blotting paper. Continue building alternate layers of newspaper and blotting paper with flowers between, until you have reached a maximum of ten layers.

Screw down the press as firmly as possible, and leave it in a warm place for about six to eight weeks – without looking inside!

• Once your pressed flowers are ready to use, store them in a warm, dark place so that the petals don't fade or re-absorb moisture, which would cause the flowers to turn moldy. Cellophane-fronted paper bags or blotting paper folders work well for storage.

Fresh, dried, and pressed flowers make lovely gifts. Collect baskets, ribbons, and doilies in advance.

Wedding anniversaries

Flowers make the ideal gift for wedding anniversaries. For an especially thoughtful gift, you could incorporate an anniversary token into your bouquet or arrangement. Listed below are the traditional materials from which an anniversary gift should be made.

1st – Paper	9th – Pottery or willow	25th – Silver
2nd – Cotton	10th – Tin	30th – Pearl
3rd – Leather	11th – Steel	35th – Coral
4th – Fruit or flowers	12th – Silk or linen	40th – Ruby
5th – Wood	13th – Lace	45th – Sapphire
6th – Sugar or iron	14th – Ivory	50th – Gold
7th – Wool or copper	15th – Crystal	55th – Emerald
8th – Pottery or bronze	20th – China	60th – Diamond

Suppliers

The following stores and companies all offer a mail order service.

Aphrodisia
282 Bleecker St.
New York, NY 10014
for dried flowers, potpourri, and essential oils

Dorothy Biddle Service
Greeley, PA 18425
for florist's supplies and tools

Williams Sonoma Grande Cuisine
150 Post St.
San Francisco, CA 94108
for Christmas crackers

You may also wish to write to the author's company,
Joanna Sheen Ltd.
P.O. Box 52
Newton Abbot
Devon TQ12 4QH
United Kingdom
Fax 011 44 1626 872405
for a catalog detailing her range of oils, dried flowers, and pressed flowers and the courses she offers. Christmas crackers similar to those shown on pages 104–105 can also be obtained through her company. Inquiries and orders must be accompanied by the appropriate international postal reply coupons.

$\mathcal{I}$ndex

ACKNOWLEDGMENTS

Merehurst would like to thank the following for lending props for the photographs in
this book: David Robertson and Peta Weston for creating the special backgrounds;
Shirley Dupree for lending the wooden toys from her collection; and Margaret Check,
Hazel Hurst, and Nesta MacDonald, who kindly lent their lace, table linen, and dishes.